A Handbook of Discernment for Evangelical Christians Considering Ministry as a Professional Chaplain

A Handbook of Discernment for Evangelical Christians Considering Ministry as a Professional Chaplain

John Ruiz

WIPF & STOCK · Eugene, Oregon

A HANDBOOK OF DISCERNMENT FOR EVANGELICAL
CHRISTIANS CONSIDERING MINISTRY AS A PROFESSIONAL
CHAPLAIN

Copyright © 2025 John Ruiz. All rights reserved. Except for brief quotations in critical publications or reviews, no part of this book may be reproduced in any manner without prior written permission from the publisher. Write: Permissions, Wipf and Stock Publishers, 199 W. 8th Ave., Suite 3, Eugene, OR 97401.

Resource Publications
An Imprint of Wipf and Stock Publishers
199 W. 8th Ave., Suite 3
Eugene, OR 97401

www.wipfandstock.com

PAPERBACK ISBN: 979-8-3852-3581-0
HARDCOVER ISBN: 979-8-3852-3582-7
EBOOK ISBN: 979-8-3852-3583-4

VERSION NUMBER 020325

Unless otherwise indicated, all Scripture quotations are taken from the New Revised Standard Version Bible, copyright © 1989 National Council of the Churches of Christ in the United States of America. Used by permission. All rights reserved worldwide.

This book is dedicated to the trailblazers and wildflowers who have taught me, mentored me, and blessed my life.

Contents

Introduction | ix

Chapter 1
A Blessing to the Nations and the Implications
for Professional Chaplaincy | 1

Chapter 2
Implications of Authenticity in Professional Chaplaincy:
A Biblical Perspective | 14

Chapter 3
The Mystery of the Trinity and Forms of Unity | 35

Chapter 4
Paradigm Shifts in the World of Professional Chaplaincy
and a Role for Evangelical Christian Chaplains | 48

Chapter 5
Living in the Mystery and Experiencing the Divine | 74

Chapter 6
Trailblazers: Interviews with Professional Chaplains | 87

Chapter 7
The Professional Chaplain as Evangelist | 92

Bibliography | 97

Introduction

THE PURPOSE OF THIS handbook is to encourage discernment for evangelical Christians who are considering ministry as a professional chaplain. The handbook illustrates practical applications of the art of chaplaincy and provides a framework for navigating entry into the profession, at both the professional and church level. The resource is also designed for teachers who instruct individuals considering professional chaplaincy. The hope is to encourage and assist evangelical Christians who feel called to the ministry of professional chaplaincy to enter into and successfully practice their ministry. The reason for the handbook is my belief and observation, working seventeen-plus years as a professional chaplain, that God is using professional chaplaincy in a multicultural reality to reach the unchurched, the minimally churched and those who are not currently having their needs met by the traditional form of church.

Ecclesial Context

I began serving as a pastor in the local church in 1995 and was ordained an elder in the United Methodist Church in 1999. I have served as a pastor in the local church for over twenty years. I currently continue to serve as a pastor to three small churches in the Zanesville, Ohio, area.

In April 2007, I began ministry as a chaplain. I completed four units of Clinical Pastoral Education (CPE) and became a board-certified chaplain (BCC) in 2015. A constant during these seventeen-plus years has been serving as an emergency department chaplain. In this role, I often serve people in times of deep emotion, pain, and grief. I am also the primary chaplain in the medical intensive care unit and the neurological intensive care unit. In these areas of the hospital, I often companion with patients and families. These medical journeys can vary greatly. During the COVID-19 pandemic, being the senior member of the staff, I was assigned a thirty-two-bed intensive care unit for COVID+ patients. My COVID-19 experience led to the writing and publication of a book titled *A Chaplain's Perspective on the 2020–2021 Pandemic: Tragedy, Resilience, Hope*.

Contemporary Foundation

During my time as a professional chaplain, it has become apparent that any person within a faith tradition based upon a belief in an absolute truth can have difficulty when entering the profession. A few examples are the Jewish believer who holds, as absolute truth, "There is no God but Yahweh"; the Catholic believer who holds, as absolute truth, "Salvation is known in and through the Church"; and the Islamic believer who holds, as absolute truth, Mohammad's teachings in the Koran. This is true as well for the evangelical Christian who holds, as absolute truth, "Jesus Saves." This is consistent with the proclamation of the World Council of Churches that the Lord Jesus Christ is "God and Savior according to the Scriptures," a foundational declaration of that body.[1]

The challenge to those whose faith is rooted in these beliefs developed in 2004 when the certification competencies, Common Standards of Professional Chaplaincy, broadened the scope within which professional chaplains serve. In the Common Standards of Professional Chaplaincy, the Association of Professional Chaplains mandated that "chaplains are to provide pastoral care that respects diversity and differences including but not limited to

---

1. Green et al., *Church from Every Tribe*, 27.

culture, gender, sexual orientation, and spiritual practices."[2] This led to the perspective summarized by Fukuyama and Sevig who understood that having a pluralistic worldview, meaning no tradition has the "corner on truth," would be a requirement to be an effective professional chaplain.[3]

The image used when considering professional chaplaincy is that of a sandbox. Originally, it was believed that a pluralistic worldview would mean everyone would be allowed in the sandbox of professional chaplaincy. However, this has not been the case and those traditions that hold to an absolute truth have had difficulty entering the "sandbox," meaning the profession of chaplaincy as a board-certified chaplain. Board certification is a requirement for many, if not most, positions in professional chaplaincy. This handbook will explore how this assumption is changing within professional chaplaincy from pluralism to authenticity in practice and personhood.

Overview of Handbook

Chapter 1, "A Blessing to the Nations and the Implications for Professional Chaplaincy," examines the logic of mission from a Christian perspective and makes a brief exploration of God's universal salvific intent. This is necessary within professional chaplaincy, which broadens the scope of ministry from participants in one's parish, church, or denomination to include all people. This scope suggests that the world is one's parish, which becomes the starting point of professional chaplaincy. The chapter then examines the biblical figure of Ananias in the book of Acts as an archetypal figure for professional chaplaincy. Finally, it offers a practical application of professional chaplains as healing agents during times of grief and loss and uses biblical imagery on grief and healing.

Chapter 2, "Implications of Authenticity in Professional Chaplaincy: A Biblical Perspective," provides an exploration of

2. Cadge and Sigalow, "Negotiating Religious Differences," 147.
3. Fukuyama and Sevig, "Cultural Diversity," 29.

God's universal salvific intent now understood through the life, death, and resurrection within the Johannine community. This chapter concludes with a discussion on marriage and LBGTQ+ issues. This discussion will lead to the reality of authenticity. The reality of authenticity brings the first foot into the sandbox of professional chaplaincy for the evangelical Christian.

Chapter 3, "The Mystery of the Trinity and Forms of Unity," dialogues with pluralism and the various ways unity is formed. The chapter explores the contributions of the Christian community in conversations concerning unity within communities and the dignity within all people. Finally, this chapter considers the need for evangelical Christians to assume their role within professional chaplaincy to assist the profession to live its own mission, and ministry, more faithfully.

Chapter 4, "Paradigm Shifts in the World of Professional Chaplaincy and a Role for Evangelical Christian Chaplains," examines the shift in professional chaplaincy from an approach that focuses on "how" a person gets better to often also include "if" a person gets better. This shift is occurring because of evidence-based research. The chapter then examines challenges for entry and practice as board-certified chaplains. The issue of authenticity will be reexamined as will the need for integrity in personhood as seen in practice by the evangelical Christian chaplain. The need for integrity in personhood by the evangelical Christian chaplain places the second foot into the sandbox of professional chaplaincy.

Chapter 5, "Living in the Mystery and Experiencing the Divine" explores distinct contributions in ministry that occur when evangelical Christians take their place in professional chaplaincy. In other words, it begins to examine the ministry that would not take place and the healing that would not occur in those being served if evangelical Christian chaplains were not present.

Chapter 6, "Trailblazers: Interviews from Professional Chaplains," includes interviews with evangelical Christians who have successfully served in the ministry of professional chaplaincy. These persons have helped blaze a trail for others to follow.

Chapter 7, "The Professional Chaplain as Evangelist," will briefly examine history and recent times to explore when God has used representative ministry as a form of evangelism. It concludes with encouragement for more evangelical Christians to enter God's vineyard of professional chaplaincy.

It should be noted, names and small details have been changed in the examples of pastoral care from the bedside to preserve confidentiality. Also, unless otherwise noted, all biblical quotations are from the New Revised Standard Version (NRSV) of the Bible.

Chapter 1

A Blessing to the Nations and the Implications for Professional Chaplaincy

"... so that you will be a blessing."
GENESIS 12:2b

GOOD NEWS IS MEANT to be shared. Throughout the Bible the good news of God is meant to be shared. When God calls Abraham, it is not only for the descendants of Abraham, but rather, it is for all the earth: "In you all the families of the earth shall be blessed" (Gen 12:3b). Therefore, God's intent is embodied by the community in mission.

God's intent has always been for all persons: "And by your offspring shall all the nations of the earth gain blessing for themselves, because you have obeyed my voice" (Gen 22:18). An inexhaustive examination of biblical texts echoing this theme of God's intent includes Gen 18:18, Gen 26:4, Gen 28:14; Ps 67:2, Ps 98:3; Isa 42:1–7, Isa 45:22, Isa 49:1–6, Isa 53, Isa 66:18; Jer 4:1–2; Zech 8:7; Matt 28:16–20; Mark 16:5; Luke 2:28–32; John 3:16–17; Rom 10:12–15; Gal 3:8–9; Phil 2:5–11; 1 Tim 2:4; and Rev 21:3.

The scholar Richard Bauckham summarizes this theme, writing,

> It was never God's intention to bless Abraham purely for his and his descendants' sake. It was never God's intention to reveal himself to Israel only for Israel's sake. It was never God's intention to base his kingdom in Zion only so that he might rule the immediate locality. God's purpose in each of these singular choices was universal; that the blessing of Abraham might overflow to all the families of the earth, that God's self-revelation to Israel might make God known to all nations, that from Zion his rule might extend to the ends of the earth.[1]

Later Bauckham speaks of the logic of mission and how the theme of mission relates to the Christian, writing, "Mission takes place between the highly particular history of Jesus and the universal goal of God's coming kingdom."[2] Veli-Matti Kärkkäinen succinctly states, "The church exists in mission."[3]

Walter Brueggemann writes concerning the logic of mission and the need for "humanity not defined by commodity." Brueggemann analyzes that "despair is the defining mark of the context for church mission in the twenty-first century" and the Christian as a "community of hope" must engage this reality.[4]

The recent article titled "Training Chaplains and Spiritual Caregivers: The Emergence and Growth of Chaplaincy Programs in Theological Education" discovered "substantial growth in chaplaincy-focused programs in theological schools in the last twenty years."[5] This article interviewed several leaders in the formation of chaplaincy programs including Jan McCormack who highlighted several unique characteristics of professional chaplains. McCormack explains, "We chaplains don't wait for people to come to us. We go to them. And we're typically working in someone else's work center."[6] Finally, the article discusses how many times individuals,

---

1. Bauckham, *Bible and Mission*, 46.
2. Bauckham, *Bible and Mission*, 84.
3. Kärkkäinen, "Ecclesiology and the Church," 28.
4. Brueggemann, *Hope for the World*, 155.
5. Cadge et al., "Training," 190.
6. Cadge et al., "Training," 192.

especially young people, who might not trust organized religion and clergy in general are willing to trust a chaplain. Therefore, moving into the future it may be chaplains who will be the primary healers to individuals in the public sphere during times of crisis.[7]

Following this logic, it may be evangelical chaplains who will be the agents of sharing the good news of Jesus Christ to those who do not know and follow Jesus. Often this is done through witness and action in times of grief and loss. Logically, for some, this might then be a person's first encounter with an act of compassion that was inspired by a relationship with God in Jesus Christ and a desire to share this good news with others.

Evangelical Christians have a necessary role within the ministry of professional chaplaincy and more importantly within the biblical witness of God's healing intent. Turning to the Bible the evangelical Christian can find a model for professional chaplaincy within Ananias who is the archetypal evangelical professional chaplain.

Ananias: The First New Testament Professional Evangelical Chaplain

Now there was a disciple in Damascus named Ananias. The Lord said to him in a vision, "Ananias." He answered, "Here I am Lord." The Lord said to him, "Get up and go to the street called Straight, and at the house of Judas look for a man of Tarsus named Saul. At this moment he is praying, and he has seen in a vision a man named Ananias come in and lay his hands on him so that he might regain his sight." But Ananias answered, "Lord, I have heard from many about this man, how much evil he has done to your saints in Jerusalem; and here he has authority from the chief priests to bind up all who invoke your name." But the Lord said to him, "Go, for he is an instrument whom I have chosen to bring my name before Gentiles and kings and before the people of Israel; I myself will

---

7. Cadge et al., "Training" 192.

> *show him how much he must suffer for the sake of my name."*
> *So Ananias went and entered the house. He laid his hands on Saul and said,*
> *"Brother Saul, the Lord Jesus, who appeared to you on your way here, has sent me so that you may regain your sight and be filled with the Holy Spirit."*
> *And immediately something like scales fell from his eyes, and his sight was restored.*
> *Then he got up and was baptized, and after taking some food, he regained his strength.*
> Acts 9:10–19

As described in this passage, Ananias demonstrates seven characteristics of a professional evangelical chaplain. First, Ananias is in mission. He is called by God for a purpose and Ananias answers the call (Acts 9:10). Second, the movement of professional chaplaincy is to go to where people reside. Ananias goes and enters the house where Saul is at, blind and in need of a healing touch (Acts 9:17). Third, professional chaplaincy is a ministry to all. Ananias is obedient and moves beyond his community to serve Saul (Acts 9:13–14). Fourth, professional chaplaincy does not always make sense. It is very difficult to explain to others what a professional chaplain does and often to the hearer it is hard to understand why anyone would want to be a professional chaplain. Initially, Ananias objects to the Lord and reminds the Lord of Saul's history and reputation (Acts 9:13–14). It would not seem logical to want to go in the name of the Lord to be a healing agent to someone who had caused so much harm and misery to the faithful followers of Jesus.

Fifth, a professional chaplain seeks to be a blessing to others. In this way, the professional chaplain seeks to be a healing agent physically, emotionally, and spiritually. Ananias touches Saul (Acts 9:17). This touch by a professional chaplain does not always occur in a physical way; however, many times holding a person's hand can be healing. Sixth, all professional chaplains are ordained clergy; therefore, there are times the professional chaplain serves in a capacity congruent with their ordination, including religious practices, rituals, and sacraments.

In his actions, Ananias is the first evangelical professional chaplain; he goes to Saul as a representative of Jesus and speaks in the name of Jesus. "So Ananias went and entered the house. He laid his hands on Saul and said, 'Brother Saul, the Lord Jesus, who appeared to you on the way here, has sent me so that you may regain your sight and be filled with the Holy Spirit" (Acts 9:17). Finally, Ananias baptized Saul.

Seventh, Ananias is largely forgotten. Throughout his travels and letters the apostle Paul does not mention Ananias by name. One can assume that the experience of Ananias in his life would have been profound to Paul; however, Paul recognizes Jesus the risen Savior, as the true active, healing agent in his life. Therefore, Paul rejoices in Christ!

Professional Chaplains as Healing Agents During Times of Grief and Loss (Biblical Imagery on Grief and Healing)

Some topics covered in Clinical Pastoral Education (CPE) include the various kinds of loss that may be experienced by patients and families. These losses can include the loss of control for a person who needs nursing home care due to physical decline, a change in career or lifestyle due to an unexpected diagnosis or amputation, the loss of identity for families of an individual with Alzheimer's disease, the time spent at the bedside of a loved one nearing death and in anticipation of death, or a parent who seeks to live after the death of a child. Biblical imagery can speak in healing ways into each of these types of situations.

A powerful biblical image during times of unexpected life transition and loss is Ps 84:1–12 and the journey through the Valley of Baca. This particular image reminds us that healing in these times is a process and a journey and reminds us of God's faithfulness and of the importance of movement in one's personal healing story.

Another biblical image is found in Isa 40:30–31: "Even youths will faint and be weary, and the young will fall exhausted;

but those who wait upon the Lord shall renew their strength, they shall mount up with wings like eagles, they shall run and not be weary, they shall walk and not faint." Life might be different due to a new diagnosis or an amputation, yet life remains beautiful and full of possibilities. This passage reminds us that where we are at a given point is not the final destination. There is the possibility of healing and of a sense of new wholeness and strength. There is hope in God who renews our strength.

G. A. Bonanno identified a path of resilience experienced when individuals continue to function and cope after times of pain, loss, and death.[8] Bonanno's work discovered four paths including chronic grief, delayed grief, recovery from grief (acceptance and improved life function), and the path of resiliency.[9] In the article "Resilience and Professional Chaplaincy: A Paradigm Shift in Focus,"[10] researcher Steven Spidell builds on Bonanno's work.

Spidell and Bonanno provide invaluable growth to the work of Elisabeth Kübler-Ross who identifies stages of grief in her seminal book *On Death and Dying*. These stages of grief include denial, anger, bargaining, depression, and acceptance.[11] Today it is widely accepted that these stages are not experienced in a linear way, rather they describe the "pool of grief," which is experienced in a more haphazard way. The awareness that grief is experienced in different ways by individuals means that the services provided by the professional chaplain are also different.

As a professional chaplain the art of chaplaincy during this time of ministry is to first identify which path an individual is accessing in their processing of the moment. The professional chaplain then seeks to educate and normalize the journey chosen by each individual. In this way, the professional chaplain attempts to normalize what each person is experiencing and educates what might be expected and possible points where additional professional help in grief recovery may be prudent. Finally, the persons

8. Bonanno, "Loss," 22–24; Bonanno, "Uses and Abuses," 753–56.
9. Bonanno, "Uses and Abuses," 753–56.
10. Spidell, "Resilience," 16–23.
11. Küebler-Ross, *On Death and Dying*.

being served by the professional chaplain may become the educators and guides for loved ones who are not present but will also experience pain, loss, and grief with the death of a loved one. Biblical imagery provides an amazing well of healing to meet these differences in coping and healing.

In his book *Journeying with Jeanette: A Love Story into the Land and Language of Alzheimer's* Robert Crick beautifully and honestly describes the many little losses experienced by his wife Jeanette and those that loved her, including her family, friends, and church community. Crick writes of the decision made "to travel with Jeanette covenantally rather than contractually."[12] Later he writes of the decision made "to be bearers of her personhood when she could no longer bear it herself."[13]

Crick's experience reminds me of the source of healing found in Ps 23, which I have often used when ministering with families during these types of extended journeys that can move into days and months and years. The decision to "dwell in the valley of the shadow of death" (Ps 23:4) with another person is always a choice. Psalm 23 provides a framework for the journey and where it ultimately leads, "and I will dwell in the house of the Lord forever" (Ps 23:6). Psalm 23 reminds us that God is with us in the midst of the journey in personal ways "The Lord is my shepherd I shall not want" (Ps 23:1). Finally, it reminds us that there will be a day where we will need to consciously journey from the valley of the shadow of death to "still waters" and allow God to renew our souls (Ps 23:2–3a). This type of imagery can be especially helpful for long-term caregivers. For Robert Crick it meant writing a book.

I remember a specific encounter with a young man in his thirties who had requested a chaplain visit. He was alert and pleasant and seemed to welcome the visit. I learned he was in the hospital due to a work-related injury. He spoke of his Christian faith and seemed to be struggling with meaning making and future goals, as he was questioning his ability to return to his former work full

---

12. Crick, *Journeying with Jeanette*, 19.
13. Crick, *Journeying with Jeanette*, 63.

time. I learned he was a landscaper and it seemed he had little support outside of his mother and a few coworker friends.

After spending some time together and building a rapport he decided to share the real reason for his request for a chaplain visit. He shared that the next day would mark the birthday of his son. I learned that his son was born ill and did not live long on this earth. I learned his son would be turning eight. He seemed to brighten when I asked the name of his son. He informed me his son's name is Shawn. There is great power in a name. I learned that after Shawn's death, he and the boy's mother (his fiancée) had broken up. He told me that he had spoken at Shawn's funeral, even though speaking in public was something he rarely did. I then perceived that he seemed stuck in his grief and seemed to have journeyed very little from Shawn's funeral in terms of meaning making, processing, moving his grief, and developing future goals.

We explored some ideas together. How might he find still waters and allow God to renew his soul? How might he move his grief in a meaningful way? He landed on the idea of planting a tree, something that seemed to be appropriate for a landscaper. Before I left, we prayed together, and he looked tangibly different. He told me he had not spoken of Shawn for a long time and the conversation seemed to encourage and equip him to move within his grief and begin to envision a future.

One of the responsibilities of chaplains is to accompany patients as they approach death. Required reading in my preparation for palliative care and hospice ministry included the book *Final Gifts: Understanding the Special Awareness, Needs, and Communications of the Dying*. The book describes Nearing Death Awareness:

> The experience of dying frequently includes glimpses of another world and those waiting in it. Although they provide few details, dying people speak with awe and wonder of the peace and beauty they see in the other place. They tell of talking with or sensing the presence of people whom they cannot see—perhaps people they have known and loved. They know, often without being

told, they are dying, and may even tell us when their death will occur.[14]

Becoming more aware and comfortable in this aspect of a person's journey from life to life can allow the professional chaplain to develop a framework for being with the loved ones of a patient nearing death. Psalm 23 and Heb 12:1–3 can be healing in normalizing the experience in the context of Christian faith so that loved ones at the bedside can be open to the possibility of final gifts. Hebrews 12:1–3 reads, "Therefore, since we are surrounded by so great a cloud of witnesses, let us lay aside every weight and sin that clings so closely, and let us run with perseverance the race that is set before us, looking to Jesus the pioneer and perfecter of our faith, who for the sake of the joy that was set before him endured the cross, disregarding its shame, and has taken his seat at the right hand of the throne of God."

Normalizing a room by moving a chair so that loved one's can hold the patient's hand, offering a warm blanket, a cup of ice water or coffee, and playing music can bring calm and allow loved ones to simply *be* with their loved one who is approaching the end of their earthly journey. There are times that normalizing the experience can lead to additional moments of healing through storytelling, prayer, and ritual. Normalizing a patient's apparent haphazard reaching and transitional gaze, where it seems that a patient is looking through you to something beyond, in the context of Christian faith and the truth of a "great cloud of witnesses that surrounds us" (Heb 12:1) can bring a "peace that passes all understanding" (Phil 4:6) and a realization that these moments dwelling at the bedside of a dying person are both some of the hardest and holiest moments a person can experience.

For some families, ritual can be healing; conducting a Protestant anointing based on James 5:14–15 can be very meaningful and healing. "Are any among you sick? They should call for elders of the church and have them pray over them, anointing them with oil in the name of the Lord. The prayer of faith will save the sick,

---

14. Callanan and Kelley, *Final Gifts*, 14–15.

and the Lord will raise them up; and anyone who has committed sins will be forgiven."

The evangelical professional chaplain who is also an ordained clergy person within their own church affiliation can gather family and loved ones for an anointing of the sick. Further, the evangelical professional chaplain can read biblical passages and pray authentically in Jesus' name. The 2019 article "Quality of Spiritual Care at the End of Life: What the Family Expects for Their Loved One" discovered that providing religious rituals such as the anointing of the sick along, with emotional support, active listening, prayer, Scripture reading, and being a physical reminder of God's presence are expected by patients and families.[15] Therefore, these types of holy and healing moments are expected by patients and families and can only be provided by the Ananias in our midst.

The book *Tuesdays with Morrie* by Mitch Albom beautifully illustrates the gifts that are often given by individuals whose health is slowly declining. The apostle Paul reminds us that "this perishable body must put on imperishability, and this mortal body must put on immortality" (1 Cor 1:53). This is always difficult for loved ones either if it occurs instantly and unexpectedly in an emergency department or over a lengthy period, as with Morrie. Albom describes his experience with Morrie who is his former professor, teacher, mentor, and friend, and through his description the reader can see Albom going through the stages of his own personal grief as he watches Morrie's slow decline. Albom also describes the "final gifts" and wisdom given by Morrie as Albom chose to travel through the valley of the shadow of death with Morrie.[16]

During my CPE training, significant time was spent discussing how a professional chaplain is to deal with those instances when the chaplain is kicked out of the room. Being kicked out of the room is not always a bad thing. In fact, it can be a way for a patient or family to exert a small amount of autonomy and control in a situation where they might feel powerless.

---

15. Heinke et al., "Quality of Spiritual Care," 159–174.
16. Albom, *Tuesdays with Morrie*.

In the hospital setting I am a part of the professional chaplains that go to every death as a standard practice. My assumption as I began my career as a professional chaplain was that families in intense grief at the death of a loved one might not want a chaplain. Experience has proven otherwise and points us to a deeper theological truth. In my seventeen-plus years as a professional chaplain, I have been called to be with families at the time of death thousands of times and I have never had a family request that I leave.

The great thinker Lancelot Andrewes (1555–1626) spoke into these moments when he preached on Lam 12:1, a verse that reads: "Is it nothing to you, all you who pass by? Look and see if there is any sorrow in my sorrow, which is brought upon me, which the Lord inflicted on the day of his fierce anger." Andrews spoke concerning the importance of recognition and presence within times of loss and grief, preaching, "It showeth that there be yet some that are touched with the sense of misery, that wish us well, and would give us ease if they could."[17] Andrews points us to the universal truth of misery experienced in unrecognized grief. In this way, the professional chaplain entering the room and stating his or her purpose, "I am chaplain John. I know this is a difficult time and I am here to give support and help with what happens next," meets the universal need of unrecognized grief.

Two situations as an emergency department chaplain stand out in the use of the healing resource of biblical imagery in these situations. First is a "soul cry." I have only heard it three or four times and it is a cry that can be recognized even if never heard before. This has occurred in sudden death situations when a loved one has somehow been able to use denial to keep themselves from imagining any possibilities not hoped for. Therefore, when told the truth of the moment there is no preparation or filter; rather a spontaneous, guttural, unfiltered cry of agony and loss emerges. It is a very difficult experience, both for the mourner and for all those present.

---

17. Lancelot Andrewes, quoted in Davis, *Wondrous Depth*, 103.

Even in the depths of grief, a source of healing can be found in Jesus' encounter with Mary Magdalene at the tomb (John 20:11–18); Mary Magdalene is so overwhelmed by her grief, she cries, "They have taken away my Lord, and I do not know where they have laid him" (John 20:13). This passage reminds us that Jesus is with us as a companion and comforter even when we are unaware due to the overwhelming grief of the moment. Jesus is eventually able to reach Mary Magdalene by simply stating her name: "Jesus said to her, Mary!" (John 20:16). Sitting with someone, lightly touching their hand or shoulder, and stating their name or asking them their name can assist a person to move from the depths of a soul cry or the cognitive fog experienced in "Mary Magdalene type grief."

Finally, the healing ministry of presence and the biblical wisdom of presence are found in the following verse from Ps 46: "Be still and know that I am God" (Ps 46:10). This tool is often used by the professional chaplain in healing ways with patients and families. I conclude with an experience that occurred on a Saturday night.

I was working a night shift and responded to a trauma alert. We learned from medics that the patient, a young woman, had been shot in the back of the head. When they rolled her over to examine the injury a game controller fell out of her hands and landed on the floor. She must have been playing a video game, which would explain the lack of defensive wounds. We were able to determine the patient's name through an ID on her person but were unable to locate any next of kin. There were many unanswered questions. Medically there was nothing that could be done. The patient's brain was swelling, and the patient was dying. She was moved to an intensive care bed in the main hospital. Police were sent back to the scene to try and find next of kin or someone who might know the patient.

A few hours later, I received a call that the mother of the patient had arrived and was at the bedside. I decided to spend a few moments to collect myself and pray. During that time, I received another call from the nurse informing me that the mother was requesting a prayer. This informed me, within a Christian framework, that the mother was traveling this darkest of valleys.

I met the mother at the bedside. She was sitting quietly and gazing lovingly at her daughter. We shared in prayer together and I asked her if it would be okay to sit with her. She agreed and I pulled up a chair on the other side of the patient's bed. She shared a few stories of the patient but mostly we sat silently, each in our own thoughts and prayers. The words of Ps 46 echoed: *"Be still and know that I am God."*

At one point I asked the mother of the patient if she would like some water or coffee and she agreed to coffee. I got two cups of coffee, one for her and one for myself. Saying very little we sat together at the bedside. When I finished my coffee, I excused myself and let her know I would be back. I wanted to give her space and let her know I could return.

When I left the room, I noticed a police officer present and learned that a suspect had been detained. The police officer was present to report when the patient died. As the morning approached, I was called back by the nurse and informed that the patient had died. I returned to the room and once again her mom and I shared in prayer in Jesus' name. She seemed to be drawing great strength from her Christian faith and trust in resurrection hope (1 Pet 1:3–4). I then assisted with decedent care questions and issues.

Spiritual Discernment Questions

1. Have you ever experienced an Ananias in your life? Explain. If not, have you ever experienced a mentor in your life? Explain
2. How might your experience influence your ministry as a professional chaplain?
3. When considering pastoral ministry in a church setting, what biblical passages and images come to mind?
4. When considering chaplaincy ministry in a variety of settings, what biblical passages and images come to mind?

Chapter 2

Implications of Authenticity in Professional Chaplaincy

A Biblical Perspective

> "The true light, which enlightens everyone, was coming into the world."
>
> JOHN 1:9

THE JOHANNINE UNDERSTANDING OF God's universal salvific will is a motif that is seen throughout the Johannine corpus (John 1:9; John 3:16–17; John 4:42; John 12:32; John 12:47; 1 John 2:1–2; 1 John 4:14). God's universal salvific intent is God's ultimate purpose. "Indeed, God did not send the Son into the world to condemn the world, but in order that the world might be saved through him" (John 3:17). Within the Johannine corpus this motif is not new. As explored in the previous chapter God's universal salvific intent is found throughout both the Hebrew Bible (Old Testament) and the New Testament. The motif of God's universal salvific will is now understood in a greater way in the Johannine corpus in the light of the life, death, and resurrection of Jesus.

The Gospel of John begins with a creation account (John 1:1–5) thus reminding the reader of earlier creation accounts known within the community. John then introduces God's universal salvific will in light of the "one who shines in the darkness" (1:5a): "The true light which enlightens everyone, was coming into the world" (1:9).

The scholar James McPolin writes, "The Word was the true light who, in coming into the world, enlightens 'every man' for, as the perfect and authentic revealer, he provides light for every man and in some mysterious way his work touches even those who do not know him."[1]

Donald Senior builds on this idea,

> To reveal God is the heart of Jesus' mission and, for John's Gospel, the key to understanding all that Jesus says and does. Jesus takes 'flesh'—that is, takes on a human nature and a human history—in order that God's consuming love for the world would be visible and comprehensible to the human world. Revealing God in Johannine terms is not the mere dissemination of information about God. What Jesus reveals is that God will not condemn the world, but that God loves the world and intends to save it (John 3:16–17). Thus, the message Jesus embodies is active, dynamic, compelling.[2]

Later Senior writes, "The return to God—not only the world but all humanity—is the final purpose of Jesus' mission in the world."[3]

The motif of God's universal salvific will is repeated throughout the Gospel of John and 1 John; therefore, all the literature of the Johannine corpus is understood as dwelling within this theme. To analyze a Johannine understanding of God's universal salvific will, three modern-day forms of interpretation will be discussed. Addressing these three issues will then allow for the hearing of the Johannine voice within the context of its original setting and meaning.

---

1. McPolin, *John*, 7.
2. Senior, *Passion of Jesus*, 16.
3. Senior, *Passion of Jesus*, 17.

The three issues to be addressed include, first, the issue of authorship; second, the use of the words antichrist, Satan, and devil; and third, the Johannine understanding of sin. First, the issue of authorship: there is no consensus among biblical scholars concerning the authorship of the corpus of Johannine literature.[4] However, a significant school of biblical scholars recognize the corpus of Johannine literature contained in the Bible includes the Gospel of John, 1 John, 2 John, and 3 John.[5] In a similar way, a significant school of biblical scholarship recognizes a different author and context for the book of Revelation.[6] This school of scholarship's long history began with Dionysius of Alexandria (d. ca. 264) who expressed doubt that John of Patmos, the author of Revelation (Rev 1:9), had written either John's epistles or the Gospel of John.[7] Understanding authorship allows the Johannine corpus and the book of Revelation to speak for themselves, thus, blessing the broader Christian family through the faithful hearing of each witness to God's faithfulness.

Second, the use of the words antichrist, Satan, and devil: Who or what do these words refer to? Within the world of scholarship, there is no agreement about who is being referred to.[8] Many scholars believe the "who" being referred to is so well known within the community that the reader does not have a need to identify themself specifically. Therefore, 1 John is written in the context of schism. Those who have fallen away from the truth were former members of the community; therefore, they do not need to be identified for the community because they are already known.[9]

---

4. See Black, *New Interpreter's Bible*, 365–66; Yarbrough, *1–3 John*, 3–7.

5. See Alexander, *Epistles of John*, 17–19; Brown, *Gospel and Epistles*, 105–8; Grayston, *New Testament*, 89; Kysar, *John*, 136–44; Williamson, *1, 2, and 3 John*, 31–51.

6. See Collins, *Crisis and Catharsis*, 25–34; Grayston, *New Testament*, 76–77; Kysar, *John*, 144–146.

7. Black, *New Interpreter's Bible*, 366.

8. See Allman, "First John 1:9," 206–9; Alexander, *Epistles of John*, 27–29; Brown, *Gospel and Epistles*, 105–8; Grayston, *New Testament*, 90.

9. See Alexander, *Epistles of John*, 27–29; Brown, *Gospel and Epistles*, 106; Grayston, *New Testament*, 90; Waters, "1 John 2:22," 29–48.

Further, a growing number of scholars understand that the writer is less concerned with the "who" and more concerned with the "what": What are those opposed to the Johannine proclamation of God's redemptive action revealed to be in the incarnate life, death, and resurrection of Jesus teaching?[10] The writer, therefore, purposefully ignores the identity of the antichrist so as to address the issue of what is being taught.

This challenge of the need for forgiveness, and therefore Christ, has occurred many times throughout history and has been addressed by many of Christianity's greatest minds. Steve Harper summarizes John Wesley, the eighteenth century theologian and evangelist with these words, "For you see, we need a Savior only if we need saving; we cannot save ourselves."[11] Within the crisis in the church being addressed in 1 John the real issue is what is being taught and the need for the redemptive act of Jesus. "This is precisely what John Wesley, in his doctrine of sin, calls us to acknowledge."[12]

Further, this purposeful, artful indeterminism is done with the recognition that separation and schism are inevitable. Therefore, the writer provides a guide for Christian communities that can be used in various settings and which then continues to proclaim and reveal God's intent, God's universal salvific will. Seen in this way, the writer is revealing how, while disagreements and even schism can be at times a threat to the Christian community, at other times can be a continued work of God aimed at God's intent and therefore a cause for celebration.

In Johannine terms the words antichrist (1 John 2:18; 1 John 2:22; 1 John 4:3), Satan, and devil (1 John 3:8; 1 John 3:10) refer to those who are teaching things that are opposed to the good news of Jesus Christ and God's atoning sacrifice through the cross of Christ. This needs to be emphasized because of imagery of Satan and the devil that developed within the Middle Ages

---

10. Alexander, *Epistles of John*, 48–51; Brown, *Gospel and Epistles*, 110–11; Grayston, *New Testament*, 89–93; Waters, "1 John 2:22," 33–34.

11. Harper, *Way to Heaven*, 23.

12. Harper, *Way to Heaven*, 23.

and culminated in Dante's *Inferno*, which was completed in AD 1314. During the Middle Ages (ca. AD 500–1500), a time of the black plague, death, despair, and seemingly constant upheaval and threats to one's very existence, devil imagery, standardized in terrifying horns and demons, provided for many Christian believers a way of explaining the world around them and a source of living with perseverance and hope. Within devil mythology is the Christian conviction that ultimately God prevails. Many believers today continue to find great strength and encouragement with this type of imagery.

Recognizing that the Johannine use of the terms antichrist, Satan, and devil differ from Middle Age mythology allows us to ask what the Johannine writer is referring to with the use of these terms. Specifically, the writer is drawing us to the sin being committed by the antichrist.

This leads us to a Johannine understanding of sin. Again, to hear the Johannine community on its own terms it is necessary to understand sin on their own terms. Within many Christian communities in Western civilization the focus on sin has been a focus on action. This can easily develop into groups that are either right with God due to their actions or wrong with God due to their actions. This then creates "in" groups (included) and "out" groups (excluded).

The fifteenth-century Christian, St. John of the Cross, challenged this type of thinking when he penned these words, "When our hearts are free from liking and judging people merely according to their natural gifts we are not held captive by external and changing charms. We are instead free to love people as they really are, and we can penetrate more easily to their core personality, their true goodness."[13]

John Wesley (1703–91) also challenged an understanding of sin focusing on human action. Harper writes concerning him, "Wesley spoke of sin in relational terms. His classic definition is that sin is 'every voluntary breach of the law of love.' At its base, sin is a broken relationship, whether that brokenness is expressed

---

13. John of the Cross, quoted in Ruth, *John of the Cross*, 46.

toward others or toward God. And it is important to note that the breach is conscious and willful."[14]

Within the Johannine understanding of sin, it is not the action of the antichrist that is sin, rather it is the teaching of the antichrist. This begs the question, What is the teaching that is defined as sin? It is the proclamation of the antichrist that claims one can be sinless (1 John 1:8; repeated in 1 John 1:10).[15] "If we say we have no sin, we deceive ourselves and the truth is not in us" (1 John 1:8). "If we say that we have not sinned, we make him a liar, and his word is not true" (1 John 1:10).

If one has attained a state of sinlessness then there is no need for God's atoning sacrifice revealed in the life, death, and resurrection of Jesus. This teaching is refuted by stating truth and expanding the implications of this truth. "My little children, I am writing these things to you so that you may not sin. But if anyone does sin, we have an advocate with the father, Jesus Christ the righteous; and he is the atoning sacrifice for our sins, and not for ours only but also for the sins of the whole world" (1 John 2:1–2). The writer returns to the centrality of this theme, "In this is love, not that we loved God but that he loved us and sent his Son to be the atoning sacrifice for our sins" (1 John 4:10). Finally, the writer emphasizes this central theme a third time, "This is the one who came by water and blood, Jesus Christ, not with water only but with water and the blood. And the Spirit is the one that testifies, for the Spirit is the truth" (1 John 5:6).

The writer then moves to reveal three distinguishing characteristics of the antichrist balanced by three distinguishing characteristics of God's faithful communities, communities that then have a role to play in God's salvific intent. The three distinguishing characteristics of the antichrist may be discerned by asking the three following questions: First, what does the community confess concerning Jesus (1 John 4:3)? Second, does the love ethic move beyond one's community, or to say it another way one's tribe (1

---

14. Harper, *Way to Heaven*, 23.

15. Brown, *Epistles of John*, 206–7; McDermond, *1, 2, 3 John*, 66; Rensberger, *1, 2, and 3 John*, 53–55.

John 2:11)? Third, where is the focus of the community (1 John 4:10)? Is the focus of the community on self or is the focus of the community on the proclamation of God and what God has done and is doing?

The three distinguishing characteristics of God's faithful community include, first, love in action, initially within the community of believers (1 John 1:10) and then extending out. Second, what is being said about Jesus. Twice it is repeated that a confession of Christ is already evidence of the indwelling of the Spirit (1 John 4:2–3a; 1 John 4:15). "By this you know the Spirit of God: every spirit that confesses that Jesus Christ has come in the flesh is from God, and every spirit that does not confess Jesus is not from God" (1 John 4:2–3a). "God abides in those who confess that Jesus is the Son of God, and they abide in him" (1 John 4:15). This two-fold repetition parallels the two-fold accusation towards the antichrist (1 John 1:8; 1 John 1:10). For the Johannine community this is the rock for unity within diversity, which is a manifestation of God's universal salvific will. Third, God's faithful community is distinguished by its focus; by contrast with the antichrist, the focus is on what God has done and is doing (1 John 4:7–11).

The writer then returns to the first distinguishing characteristic of love in action and continues to apply the implications of God's universal salvific will for the community. "And we have seen and do testify that the Father has sent his Son as the Savior of the world" (1 John 4:14). Therefore, as a result, the ethic of love in action is now extended to all, for now "those who love God must love their brothers and sisters also" (1 John 4:21) includes all persons.[16] Love, guided by the Holy Spirit, now extends to all persons since it has already been established that God has created all (John 1:5), blessed all (John 1:9), and seeks to redeem all to himself. "And I,

---

16. Alexander, *Epistles of John*, 108–114; Black, *New Interpreter's Bible*, 432; Brown, *Epistles of John*, 563–65; Loader, *Johannine Epistles*, 57–58; McDermond, *Believers' Church*, 232; Sloyan, *Walking in the Truth*, 49; Thomas, *1 John*, 237.

when I am lifted up from the earth, will draw all people to myself" (John 12:32); this passage refers to the cross of Christ.[17]

The implications of 1 John speak directly into times of disagreement and even schism within Christian communities. Seen in one light it serves as a warning for Christian communities against those who proclaim to be sinless, thus denying the need for the life, death, and resurrection of Jesus who is the atoning sacrifice and light of the world. It also provides parameters for false teachings that may develop over time.

Seen from an opposite perspective, 1 John serves as a means of recognizing and celebrating when God is expanding the community's collective understanding of God's love and salvific intent once again. First, there is cause for celebration if a community of faith that suffers a separation continues to demonstrate the distinguishing characteristics of God's faithful communities, meaning a love ethic first within one's community of believers and with God's grace extending out beyond one's community to ultimately all persons. Second, if there remains a common confession in Jesus as the Son of God and in Jesus' atoning sacrifice as God's gift of salvation. Third, if the faith community's focus remains on God and what God has done and is doing. Then God be praised! Unity within diversity is being manifested within these communities of faith. God's intent is becoming more known in heaven and on earth.

Finally, and this serves as a warning for faithful communities, love in action towards fellow believers is a distinguishing characteristic of the faithful Christian community. Further, since unity within diversity is no longer rooted in agreement then the witness of Christian communities who do not always agree yet continue to demonstrate love in action to one another serve as a beacon for the world. In other words, it becomes an intricate role that Christian communities must play in participation with God's universal salvific will.

---

17. Brown, *Gospel and Epistles*, 69; McPolin, *John*, 135–38; Senior, *Passion of Jesus*, 104; Sloyan, *John*, 159.

Marriage and LBGTQ+ Issues

In recent times the Christian family is experiencing an intense discussion and, many times, conflict over our collective understanding on marriage and LBGTQ+ issues. I will begin with a birds-eye view of various perspectives on marriage. For the purpose of this discussion, I will address three perspectives and highlight theological truths being uplifted and lived out within each community.

First, marriage is understood as a sacred union between one man and one woman. This understanding is rooted in the gospels of Matt 19:4-7 and Mark 10:6-9. "He answered, 'Have you not read that the one who made them from the beginning 'made them male and female' and said, 'For this reason a man shall leave his father and mother and be joined to his wife, and they shall become one flesh? So they are no longer two, but one flesh. Therefore, what God has joined together, let no one separate'" (Matt 19:4-7). Within this perspective the teaching on marriage is shocking because it is placed as coming directly from Jesus. Further, Jesus is teaching an understanding on marriage that is contrary to the understanding of the society of Jesus' day. In Jesus' day polygamy was still practiced in Roman culture and in some Jewish communities. Polygamy was a foundational practice within a patriarchal society. After all, Solomon had many wives.

The question then develops, Why is Jesus teaching something new? What are the implications? A traditional understanding would consider Jesus to be elevating women in a shift from polygamy to monogamy. Further, there is an elevation of the role of father as caretaker of the children. This can be seen on a practical level where there are simply less hands to care for the needs of the children in a monogamous marriage than in a polygamous relationship. A traditional theological perspective within the voices of the Christian family would center around God's love, for the Bible is littered with biblical writers using familial relationships as ways of understanding God's love for us. An inexhaustive list of biblical passages uplifting God's love for us in familial ways includes Isa 49:15, Isa 66:13; Jer 31:3; Ps 57:1, Ps 91:1-2, Ps 103:13; Matt

6:7–14, Matt 7:7–11; Luke 15:11–32; 1 John 2:1–2, 1 John 2:28, and 1 John 3:1. This train of thought continues in considering that the closest we can get to the love God has for us is in the love we experience in familial relationships.

A second understanding of marriage is also understood as a sacred union between one man and one woman. This understanding would agree with all that is above. Further, this voice within the Christian family finds its center in the biblical truths of transformation, redemption, and new life in Christ. For within this perspective of the Christian family sexual relationships outside of the marital status of one man and one woman is considered a sin. Further, sexual encounters that differ in expression from one man and one woman would also be understood as a sin. The good news is this voice of the Christian family proclaims the innate value of each person since God is the creator of life, transformation, and redemption, and new life is offered to all as a gift of a right relationship with God.

A third understanding of marriage in recent times within the Christian family challenges both the perspectives discussed above. This voice within the Christian family challenges both the notion of marriage only being understood as a union between one man and one woman and the understanding of monogamy as a traditional norm. The theological understanding of this perspective within the Christian family looks to science and the growing awareness that some people are born sexually ambiguous and others are born with natural inclinations that are not heterosexual. The theological underpinning within this voice of the Christian family centers around the biblical truths known in the creation accounts: "God is love" (1 John 4:8b), and "For where two or three are gathered in my name, I am there among them" (Matt 18:20). This perspective can be seen in T-shirts proclaiming, "Love is Love." This voice within the Christian family would challenge traditional understandings on marriage with the question, Is God expanding our collective understanding of God's love once again?

Implications for the Christian Family

It is easy to recognize that these different understandings within the Christian family cannot stand within the confines of one denomination or church. In fact, it is likely that this type of relationship would do harm to one another since the church would be limited to earthly understandings and structures that are based on human forms of authority and power. Limited to these resources, the choice to weaponize LBGTQ+ issues by voices on various sides of the discussion has impacted many of the voices in the Christian family in painful ways that do not reflect unity within diversity rooted in God's love and God's universal salvific will.

Schism seen in this regard can be understood as a continued work of God and God's reflection for the Christian family and human race. This is not new within Christian history. One example comes to mind: for many, the Protestant Reformation is not understood as a bad thing but rather as a way that God was and is acting to do something more. In this regard, the development and growth of an ecumenical spirit is a continuing light for the world and a testimony of unity within diversity.

God prodding us to understand, respect, love and find harmonize with various voices who uplift biblical truth and share a common confession in Jesus Christ is cause for rejoicing. How God fits all this together as one body, one human family, is by God's wisdom and God's salvific will.

Universalism and Johannine Theology

It is important to recognize God's universal salvific intent does not mean universalism within Johannine theology. Oxford American Dictionary defines universalism as "a person who believes that all humankind will eventually be saved."[18] This negates the need for God's grace and the atonement on the cross. This is not consistent with Johannine theology. James McPolin writes, concerning judgment and John 5:19–30,

---

18. *Oxford American Dictionary*, 2nd ed. (2008), s.v. "universalism."

But there is also an obverse side of "eternal life" in the Fourth Gospel which is called "judgment." This, however, is not an action of God by which He discriminates between good and evil; neither is it a positive action of God or of Jesus. Rather, it is what happens to a man when he deliberately rejects Jesus and the life-giving communion He offers. Besides, it is not a power of the Father or of Jesus as distinct from their power to give life, but it is a self-deserved reality, an action by which man condemns (judges) himself in rejecting Jesus. Thus "judgment" is self-condemnation, man's refusal of life either now or "on the last day" (John 5:24, 5:29 and 11:24). Yet Jesus has power to give life and to "judge" in so far as He reveals God and offers life so that a division takes place before Him: some believe, others reject Him and "judge" or condemn themselves (John 3:16–31). There is also a "resurrection of judgment" (that is, of final self-condemnation) at the end for those who have done evil (5:29).[19]

Witness to the World

Imagine the celebration of schism where various Christians, firmly rooted in confession and the need of God (Father, Son, and Holy Spirit), pray together and worship together, representing one Body in Christ; communities of faith that join in Jesus' invitation to dine at the table and to share the body and blood of Christ; believers who can join on special occasions like Holy Thursday, Easter sunrise service, or service on Christmas Eve gather for ecumenical worship; fellow Christian disciples who, at times, and when possible work together in situations like providing healthcare, disaster relief, community service, and education.

Imagine communities of Christian believers who intentionally seek to change the tone of conversation and dialogue found so often within the world, American society, and even within the church from confrontation to respect—respect not for a rival or

---

19. McPolin, *John*, 57–59,

an enemy, rather for a fellow disciple living out their faith as God is calling them. In this way, Christian communities can challenge dualistic forms of identifying communities. For dualistic forms of identifying communities are based on either/or, in/out, woke / not woke, conservative/progressive, good/evil ways of identifying themselves and others.

God is bigger than one thought or perspective fits all. God is not confined to dualistic forms of thinking. God is known more fully within the family of God devoutly living out their faith in various denominations rather than a single denomination. God is understood more completely through the choir of the Trinity than the voice of the most brilliant soloist.

A Christian witness of unity within diversity through denominations, home churches, and the broader Christian family is a faithful witness to the gospel of Jesus Christ. A witness of understanding, dignity, respect, harmony (not always agreement), and love by disciples of Jesus Christ is a light of coexistence to the world. It is the family of believers functioning as salt in God's kingdom (Matt 5:13). Therefore, it is a witness that becomes an embodiment of hope for the world.

Implications for Professional Chaplaincy

Maintaining an understanding of the mystery of the Trinity provides a framework for holding the concept of unity within diversity within various communities. The mystery of the Trinity reminds us that God is always more than we can comprehend. This is an exciting way to live. The prophet Isaiah spoke of this truth when he wrote, "As the heavens are higher than the earth, so are my ways higher than your ways, and my thoughts than your thoughts" (Isa 55:9).

Professional chaplains are called to serve all people. Further, the heart of chaplaincy is presence and representation not proclamation and conversion. Understanding the dignity and blessedness of each individual person is natural for many evangelical

Christians (and most Christians in general) because of the firm belief that God creates all human life as a visible act of God's love.

In this way, the evangelical Christian can be with and serve all persons by being an authentic and compassionate presence. At the same time, in truth, no person and no church or denomination could authentically represent each of the three understandings concerning marriage. It may be humanly possible to understand each perspective, to respect each perspective, and even to love each perspective. Therefore, it is humanly possible to understand, respect, and love individuals who dwell in each understanding of marriage. Yet it is not humanly possible to authentically represent each understanding concerning marriage.

At the same time, God's ways are higher than our ways. Therefore, it is possible that the triune God can be present in each understanding of marriage. Unity within diversity is the essence of the Trinity; therefore it can be a foundation for human community within times of human differences and disagreements. Professional evangelical chaplains are well suited to represent unity within diversity within the many and various settings that professional chaplaincy occurs. In this way, evangelical Christians serving as professional chaplains may serve as a source of community, harmony, and respect in the work settings where they serve.

Summary

To summarize and illustrate a Johannine perspective of God's universal salvific will, unity within diversity, and how it interacts with the world, I conclude with a sermon titled, "Widening Circles of Love." The scripture text for the sermon is 1 John 4:7–21.

> Beloved, let us love one another, because God is love; everyone who loves is born of God and knows God. Whoever does not love does not know God, for God is love. God's love was revealed among us in this way: God sent his only Son into the world so that we might live through him. In this is love, not that we loved God but that he loved us and sent his Son to be the atoning sacrifice for

our sins. Beloved, since God loves us so much, we also ought to love one another. No one has ever seen God; if we love one another, God lives in us, and his love is perfected in us. By this we know that we abide in him and he in us, because he has given us of his Spirit. And we have seen and do testify that the Father has sent his Son as the Savior of the world. God abides in those who confess that Jesus is the Son of God, and they abide in God. So we have known and believe the love that God has for us. God is love, and those who abide in love abide in God, and God abides in them. Love has been perfected among us in this: that we may have boldness on the day of judgment, because as he is, so are we in this world. There is no fear in love, but perfect love casts out fear; for fear has to do with punishment, and whoever fears has not reached perfection in love. We love because he first loved us. Those who say, "I love God," and hate their brothers and sisters, are liars: for those who do not love a brother and sister whom they have seen, cannot love God whom they have not seen. The commandment we have from him is this: those who love God must love their brothers and sisters also.

Widening Circles of Love

What does it mean, "Those who love God must love their brothers and sisters also" (v. 21)? What would this look like? What would a characteristic of God's illuminating love be like?

We might seek the wisdom of the apostle Paul for the understanding of these questions; we might understand the moments apostle Paul exhorts persons to "clothe yourself with the Lord Jesus Christ" (Col 3:12–14) or to be "imitators of Christ" (Eph 5:1a) were instances when Paul was suggesting one might attempt to illuminate characteristics of Christ.

One characteristic Jesus illuminated was persistent kindness, even to one's enemies. One only needs to remember the words of Jesus on the cross, "Father, forgive them; for they do not know what they are doing" (Luke 23:34a). It is this aspect of love that

Jesus reveals to the world through his life, death, and resurrection: persistent kindness even to one's enemies.

Paul is an example of someone who attempted to clothe himself with Christ (1 Cor 11:1). When Paul was known as Saul, he was a persecutor of the Christians. He sought to wipe out Christianity (Acts 7:54—8:3). How could he then broaden his circle of love to those Christians he persecuted? It was through his personal conversion and the revelation of the divinity of Christ given to him on that Damascus Road (Acts 9:1–20). Through this experience he was able to broaden his circle of love, his circle of persistent kindness, and to advocate and broaden these circles to the gentiles and all the way to the ends of the known earth.

Could it be that by attempting to imitate God's revelation of love, as known through Jesus Christ, that Paul was inspired to widen his realm of persistent kindness, his realm of love?

Giovanni Bernardone was born in 1211, in a little town in Italy, into a world of moderate comfort. His father was a prosperous merchant. What happened in this man's life to change his realm of kindness to include lepers and the poor? To extend his message of love to those outside his little town, who had grown accustomed, amused, and maybe even a little inspired by this man, to areas where people thought of him as a fool and treated him with reproach?[20]

What inspired this man, more widely known as St. Francis of Assisi, to extend his circle of love to such a great extent that it inspired the Christian church of his day to examine itself? Could it be that by attempting to imitate God's revelation of love, as known in Jesus Christ, that St. Francis was inspired to widen his realm of persistent kindness, his realm of persistent love?

Harriet Tubman was a woman of great courage and resources. Born a slave, she would risk her life to find freedom. But that is not the most amazing thing about this woman's story. She would go back to a slave south where, if caught, she would have been killed. She went back to help others find freedom. Even after she had helped her own children escape to freedom, she continued to

20. Peattie, "Everybody's Saint," 206–213.

return to help other slaves she did not even know. What could have inspired such action, such giving of herself to other oppressed people? Could it be that by attempting to imitate God's revelation of love, as known in Jesus Christ, Harriet Tubman was inspired to widen her realm of persistent kindness, her realm of persistent love?

Rev. Dr. Martin Luther King Jr. sought to peacefully end the injustice of segregation. He experienced beatings, jail (on more than one occasion), and death threats. He lived through years of struggle in pursuit of justice and change. Yet, he did not meet the difficulties and frustrations he experienced with a fist and a cry for revenge and violence but instead clung to a steadfast conviction of nonviolence and peace.

Could it be that by attempting to imitate God's revelation of love, as known in Jesus Christ, that Rev. Dr. Martin Luther King Jr. was inspired to widen his realm of persistent kindness, his realm of persistent love?

Florence was an English woman who in 1854 chose to leave her life of comfort to help develop efficient, caring nurses during the Crimean War. What inspired this woman to leave her sheltered life of comfort and to travel to a distant land to assist the wounded and dying? To lend support at a time when filth and limited medical practices were the norm? To change the perception and expectations of an entire profession? To impart dignity to those who were suffering? As one man put it in a letter home, "Before she came there was 'cussin and swearing,' but after that it was as holy as a church."[21]

What inspired this woman known as Florence Nightingale? Could it be that by attempting to imitate God's revelation of love, as known through Jesus Christ, that Florence Nightingale was inspired to widen her realm of persistent kindness, her realm of persistent love?

These are examples of individuals widening their realm of persistent kindness even to those who persecuted them. But what would be the opposite behavior? What could be the result if we

21. Andrews, "Soldiers Angel," 551–56.

decide that there are those who no longer belong to our realm of love? Who no longer deserves our persistent kindness?

Isn't that what occurred eighty-five years ago, when it was decided that those of a Jewish religion, people who did not possess the sought-after characteristics of blond hair and blue eyes no longer deserved to be treated with persistent kindness? Thereby opening the possibility to treat other people with brutality?

Could it be that a similar notion to exclude another from one's realm of love, one's realm of persistent kindness, may have occurred in 1994 in Rwanda, where tribal violence resulted in the deaths of hundreds of thousands? Could it be that a similar notion to exclude another from one's realm of love may have occurred in Bosnia and Kosovo from 1998 to 1999, when nationalistic fervor and the misuse of religious heritage resulted in human tragedy? Could the terror and death experienced more recently in Iraq and Syria from the emergence of ISIS, built on a narrow ideology of Islamic fundamentalism and jihadism, occurred due to the understanding that those who were not like-minded did not deserve to be treated with love and persistent kindness? Could it be that a quest for power and empire building has led to the exclusion of others from one's realm of love and persistent kindness, resulting in the brutality of war and the exclusion of the people of Ukraine from simply living and existing?

The United States is not innocent of excluding other people from our realm of persistent kindness. We need only remember the historic and ongoing treatment of Native Americans. We need only remember the reality and ongoing legacy of slavery and the questionable historical treatment of immigrant populations. And I am sure if we searched our minds we could come up with more examples of instances when one people has determined that another does not need to be included in one's realm of persistent kindness, one's realm of persistent love.

But what does that mean for us today? What relevance can this have for us in the communities we are a part of?

Who do we find difficult to include in our realms of kindness and love? Is it a person of a different race? Someone who looks different? Someone who thinks differently than I do? Persons of a different sexual orientation? People who speak a different language? Could it be someone who worships differently than myself? A person from a different political ideology? The possibilities seem endless. For each of us there are those who simply are more difficult to include within our realm of love and kindness. There are simply those who we are more comfortable being around and more at ease talking to. Others seem difficult to approach, so we simply avoid them.

Acknowledging with honesty and humility our humanity and the limitations we have enables us to be free to ask for God's help. It is in this human response to God's saving and atoning action in Jesus that we receive the gift of the Holy Spirit that then allows us to see, dream with, and live in community with others that we were not able to extend kindness to previously.

Who can we think of, what person, what group of people could we attempt through God's inspiration to include in our realm of love and persistent kindness?

Christ calls us to widen our realm of love and kindness. Through God's inspiration we can include those we now exclude. We must seek the help of the Lord in this endeavor and raise those currently outside our realm of love and persistent kindness to God in prayer.

Finally, to live a new life in Christ and to broaden our realm of love and persistent kindness is a life-long journey. It is a struggle, not an overnight transformation. It requires our effort, our prayers, and our trust in God.

One more idea: this is not about a passivity that enables the status quo. To this understanding, I would redirect our attention back to the apostle Paul, St. Francis of Assisi, Harriet Tubman, Rev. Dr. Martin Luther King Jr., Florence Nightingale, and those like them, for example, St. Stephen, Mother Teresa, Bishop Tutu, Anne Sullivan, Albert Schweitzer, Henri Nouwen, Oscar Romero, Corrie Ten Boom and countless others who have broadened their realms of love and kindness in glorious and inspirational ways. These people were not passive but actively demonstrated their faith and changed the lives of those privileged to know them. They challenged the status quo of their day and culture and made the world a better, more humane world because of their conviction and their life witness.

Finally, I would like to share an image that I believe seeks to move us from tolerance of another to treating another with dignity, respect, persistent kindness, and love. The modern-day thinker Esau McCaulley gives this image in his book *Reading While Black: African American Biblical interpretations as an Exercise in Hope*,

> God sees the creation of a community of different cultures united by faith in his Son as a manifestation of the expansive nature of his grace. This expansiveness is unfulfilled unless the differences are seen and celebrated, not as ends unto themselves, but as particular manifestations of the power of the Spirit to bring forth the same holiness among different peoples and cultures for the glory of God.[22]

May we, like these great illuminators of the faith, demonstrate a ministry that includes a broadening of God's love through a spirit of persistent kindness and love in new and creative ways. For "those who love God must love their brothers and sisters also" (1 John 4:21).

Spiritual Discernment Questions

1. The Bible presents two perspectives on sin. This chapter presented a relational concept of sin. Another perspective is action oriented and develops out of Scripture like the Ten Commandments (Exod 20:1–17). Which concept of sin seems more natural to you?

2. This chapter presents three perspectives on the LBGTQ+ community and Christian marriage. In which perspective do you reside?

---

22. McCaulley, *Reading While Black*, 106–7.

3. Professional chaplains must serve all people. How would your perspective influence the way you serve those who have a different perspective on Christian marriage?

Chapter 3

The Mystery of the Trinity and Forms of Unity

> "As the heavens are higher than the earth,
> so are my ways higher than your ways,
> and my thoughts than
> your thoughts."
>
> Isaiah 55:9

THIS CHAPTER WILL EXPLORE the contributions of the Christian community in conversations concerning unity within communities and dignity within all people. To do so, first it will explore the gifts found in the mystery of the Trinity. Second, it will offer a discussion concerning how these gifts within the Trinity speak into current challenges within professional chaplaincy. Third, it will explore biblical imagery concerning forms of unity. Fourth and finally, it will consider the need for evangelical Christians to assume their role within professional chaplaincy to assist the profession to live into its own mission and ministry more fully.

The Mystery of the Trinity

This exploration into the gifts found in the mystery of the Trinity does not claim to be an exhaustive exploration. Rather, it seeks to take seriously the thoughts of theologians like Janos D. Pasztor, a professor of theology in Debrecen, Hungary. Pasztor writes,

> It is Trinitarian theology that gives us the tools for critical examination of the ideas and practices of the church and its mission, past and present. Wherever this way of thinking prevails, creation, matter, history, and culture are taken seriously. Wherever it is missing, the way is open for all kinds of false views about the world and about the nature of the church and its mission. Trinitarian theology could have served—and in many cases it has served—to render help for critical self-examination, correction, and reconstruction of the life and mission of the church.[1]

Experience has taught that many times the implications and depth of the Trinity are very limited within local churches. This experience may include an occasional singing the hymn "Holy, Holy, Holy" by Reginald Heber (d. 1826). Occasionally it may include the recitation of the Nicene or the Apostle's Creeds. However, the implications of these words within God's salvific will and the various forms of community that might arise are rarely explored.

To begin a brief exploration of the Trinity and how it pertains to forms of unity I turn to Robert Kress and the article titled "Unity in Diversity: Toward an Ecumenical Perichoresic Kenotic Trinitarian Ontology." Kress draws upon the classic theological insight of unity within diversity and diversity within unity. He then relates this to the church universal, the "One Church of the One God whose oneness is not monistic but communal."[2]

In his book *The Beautiful Community: Unity, Diversity and the Church at Its Best*, Irwyn L. Ince Jr. examines how the Trinity

---

1. Janos D. Pasztor, quoted in Brueggemann, *Hope for the World*, 146.
2. Kress, "Unity in Diversity," 70.

affects our understanding of ethnicity. Ince focuses on the Christian church in the United States.

> Far from a dry, secondary, unimportant technical doctrine, God as Trinity—unity in diversity, diversity in unity—is the heartbeat of the Christian faith.[3]

Later, Ince relates the Trinity and its relationship to the human community:

> For humanity to be the image of God, it must embody beautiful community-unity in diversity, diversity in unity. If God displays his beauty in his Trinitarian life, we should expect that beauty to be reflected in the humanity that images him. While each person is royalty, we find the fullest expression of the image in community.[4]

Ince summarizes his argument: "Our theology of reconciliation is Trinitarian."[5] Marianne Maye Thompson, in her article titled "The Gospel of John and Early Trinitarian Thought: The Unity of God in John, Irenaeus and Tertullian," provides insight into Irenaeus's thought. Thompson writes concerning Irenaeus (AD 130–202) and his struggles with early Gnosticism, which sought to demote the Creator God to a secondary and inferior status, "Irenaeus combats the Gnostics who wished to sever the God who created from the God who saves."[6] In this way, Irenaeus's understanding of the coequality of the Trinity frees us from dualistic thinking.

Kevin Giles emphasizes that "diversity is of the nature of the church, not a sin to be overcome.... [Communion] reflects the unity within diversity inherent in the divine Trinity of persons that in an analogous way should characterize the life of the church in its local, regional, international, and universal dimension. The fellowship does not aim to overcome all diversity, but rather to

---

3. Ince, *Beautiful Community*, 37.
4. Ince, *Beautiful Community*, 55.
5. Ince, *Beautiful Community*, 88.
6. Thompson, "Early Trinitarian Thought," 155.

embrace it in dynamic, relational, and growing bond of love and understanding."[7]

Contributions from Professional Chaplaincy

In 2004, the Common Standard of Professional Chaplaincy broadened the scope within which professional chaplains serve. In the Common Standard of Professional Chaplaincy, the Association of Professional Chaplains mandates that "chaplains are to provide pastoral care that respects the diversity and differences including but not limited to culture, gender, sexual orientation, and spiritual and religious practices."[8] This led to the perspective summarized by Fukuyama and Sevig where it was believed that having a pluralistic worldview, meaning no one tradition has the "corner on truth" would be a requirement to be an effective professional chaplain.[9]

This shift in scope within the world of professional chaplaincy has led to wonderful contributions and difficult challenges. The contribution is the way the scope of service has forced chaplains to grow in personal ways and develop in professional ways to engage in the art of chaplaincy at the bedside, in "real time."

When I am describing professional chaplaincy to my colleagues who live out their ministry in local church environments, I begin with the differences between a pastoral care visit and a spiritual care encounter. Within a pastoral care visit there is an unspoken structure. First, the visitor is the patient's pastor or a representative from the church; therefore there is a sense of familiarity. Second, with a pastoral care visit the pastor or church representative will give some words of encouragement. Third, in some capacity (and this can vary) the visitor will draw closer to God in a more formal way through prayer and/or Bible reading.

Within a spiritual care encounter the encounter begins the same way every time. The professional chaplain is a non-anxious,

---

7. Giles, *What on Earth?*, 202.
8. Cadge and Sigalow, "Religious Differences," 147.
9. Fukuyama and Sevig, "Cultural Diversity," 29.

compassionate presence who can keep their head (meaning maintain rational, cognitive thinking) when often the patient and/or people they are serving cannot maintain rational, cognitive thinking. There are times this is all that the professional chaplain can provide due to the intensity of the moment and the emotional capability of the patient and/or people being served. There are times this presence itself can be an effective and healing spiritual care encounter.

At the same time, the art of chaplaincy draws upon extensive training in active listening, empathetic listening, and family dynamics theory, which assist the professional chaplain. These tools are used because the professional chaplain is also trying to assist the patient and/or people being served to draw forth within themselves whatever has given their lives hope, meaning, and strength in the past. Finally (and this is a key distinction between local church ministry and ministry as a professional chaplain), the professional chaplain must be open to however the patient and/or people being served answer the question of what gives their lives hope, meaning, and strength.

Current Challenges Experienced by Pluralism

Pluralism is defined as "the existence or toleration in society of a number of different ethnic groups, cultures, and beliefs."[10] A focus on pluralism has created challenges in the world of professional chaplaincy for those persons who maintain a faith perspective that holds to an absolute truth. One example would be the experience of evangelical Christians. Dr. Michael Elmore conducted a review of the challenges and difficulties experienced by many evangelical professional chaplains within their chaplaincy ministry. The result of these findings is reviewed in his dissertation, "Discovering an Evangelical Theology of Chaplaincy."

In his research, Elmore received responses from 180 evangelical professional chaplains. His findings discovered that

10. *Oxford American Dictionary*, 2nd ed. (2008), s.v. "pluralism."

approximately half of those responding reported feeling pressured to compromise their beliefs,[11] and roughly 66 percent of 119 professional chaplains reported encountering bias against evangelical professional chaplains.[12] Finally, Elmore discovered that 38 percent of the 180 evangelical professional chaplains who responded, or sixty-four evangelical professional chaplains believed their only option was to recuse themselves from providing spiritual care in their current setting or form of ministry.[13]

I have served in the United Methodist Church for over thirty years and have both seen this challenge around me and experienced it personally. In the year 2000 at the General Conference (an event that occurs every four years) the bishop of Liberia, Arthur F. Kulah, gave a message to the church entitled "The Authority of the Church." My point is not to agree or disagree with his message but instead to reflect upon how quickly his message has been dismissed, rejected, and vilified by large portions of the church.

This has occurred because Bishop Kulah took a traditional approach to the issue of homosexuality. Bishop Kulah balanced the inherent dignity of all persons stating, "Homosexuals too bear the image of God, and the grace of God is available to and sufficient for them."[14] He then conveyed his perspective rooted in his understanding of biblical authority that homosexual practice is sexually immoral and therefore outside of Christian teaching. To dismiss his thought as somehow "primitive" is a form of paternalism. To try and force Bishop Kulah (and African thinkers like him) to change his belief by withholding church funds would be a form of ideological colonization.

The issue of ideological colonialism was addressed by the church in October 2015 and reported in the article "African Bishops Throw Swift Punch at 'Ideological Colonization.'" The article reported on Pope Francis's concerns about ideological colonization—a colonization "in which Western nations have

11. Elmore, *Theology of Chaplaincy*, 128–29.
12. Elmore, *Theology of Chaplaincy*, 128–29.
13. Elmore, *Theology of Chaplaincy*, 125–26.
14. Kulah, "Authority," 10.

made acceptance of legislature favoring gay rights and 'marriage' contingent on receiving financial aid."[15]

More recently, the relatively new phenomena of "cancel culture," which seeks to silence and/or demonize thought can be seen as an outgrowth of ideological colonization since it affirms the superiority of one thought over others. Several instances of the misuse of power and ideological colonization happened within the schism that recently occurred within the United Methodist Church and the new Global Methodist Church. Thomas Lambrecht in the articles "Violations in Central Congo" and "East Angola Controversy" describes several examples of ideological colonization that occurred during the schism.

Why might pluralism struggle with the inclusion of those who hold an absolute truth, including the evangelical Christian professional chaplain? Why might pluralism struggle with paternalism and colonialist thought when it is contrary to its own stated goal? How might the evangelical Christian professional chaplain speak into these challenges? How might the evangelical Christian professional chaplain assist the field of professional chaplaincy and the world at large to live into its stated goal of coexistence more faithfully?

One possibility is to draw attention to the reliance and misuse of stage theories within Christian faith development. When I was in seminary (1993–96) the book *Faith Development and Pastoral Care: Theology and Pastoral Care*, written by James W. Fowler, was popular with many professors and students. This book was originally written in 1987. Nearly twenty years later during my Clinical Pastoral Education these ideas and theories were taught once again.

Fowler developed seven stages of faith and human becoming. These stages include what he terms Primal Faith, Intuitive-Projective Faith, Mythic-Literal Faith, Synthetic-Conventional Faith, Individualistic-Reflective Faith, Conjunctive Faith, and Universalizing Faith.[16] Fowler's intent in describing these stages was to find a

15. Harris, "African Bishops."
16. Fowler, *Faith Development*, 53–78.

way to group people and therefore best serve each group of people. However, it has not always been lived out as intended.

A problem occurs when we begin to rate these stages as one being over or better than another. For example, if a person believes they have "attained" the stage of Conjunctive Faith, then it would be easy to dismiss those people and ideas that are "below" them. While this is contrary to Fowler's thought, in practical terms it does frequently occur.

Have you ever been in a room when the speaker suddenly changes their voice to "mimic" another group of people? Perhaps the individual suddenly begins speaking with an Asian, African American, Hispanic, or Appalachian accent. This can be a subtle way of dividing and rating people, creating a very difficult work environment for the person who is part of the "accent" group.

I have experienced this during my ministry on several occasions, both as a pastor in the local church and as a professional chaplain. These are situations where it appears as if the speaker (at times the person in a leadership or teaching role) is placing themselves above another group of people. This division is not the goal of church ministry and professional chaplaincy; however, in practice it can happen.

Robert K. Atkin spoke into the challenge of Fowler's theory and the possibility that it could become a way of separating and dividing groups in a hierarchical manner. Atkin writes,

> Nobody wants to be at a low stage. All western life is geared to advancement: the promotion at work; the passing of education qualifications; moving up a year at school; buying a bigger house. Only in the kingdom of God do we see the counter to this—where we are encouraged to consider others better than ourselves and choose the lower position in life rather than the higher. Implicit in Fowler's theory is the notion that the next stage is better than the former.[17]

This is a similar challenge as that which was experienced by Irenaeus when some gnostic thinkers were "rating God" with their

---

17. Atkin, "Critical Review," para. 13.

demotion of the Creator to the status of secondary deity. In this case some argued that God be understood in stages where a saving God was superior to a God of creation.[18]

In another passage, the Bible records Jesus confronting the apostles when they were arguing over who was the greatest among them. It is recorded that Jesus brought a child among them and said, "Whoever welcomes this child in my name welcomes me, and whoever welcomes me welcomes the one who sent me; for the least among all of you is the greatest" (Luke 9:46–48).

In 2000 Fowler updated his work in the book *Becoming Adult, Becoming Christian: Adult Development and Christian Faith*. In this book Fowler addresses the misuse of rating one stage of faith development over another. Fowler writes,

> The crucial point to be grasped is that the image of human completion or wholeness offered by faith development theory is not an estate to be attained or a stage to be realized. Rather, it is a way of being and moving, a way of being on pilgrimage.[19]

Later, Fowler concludes,

> The goal, however, is not for everyone to reach the stage of universalizing faith. Rather, it is for each person or group to open themselves, as radically as possible—within the structures of their present stage or transition—to synergy with Spirit. The dynamics of that openness—and the extraordinary openings that come with "saving Grace"—operate as a lure and power toward ongoing growth and partnership with the Spirit and in the direction of universalizing faith.[20]

---

18. Thompson, "Early Trinitarian Thought," 36.
19. Fowler, *Becoming Adult*, 60.
20. Fowler, *Becoming Adult*, 60.

Biblical Images on Unity

This chapter has focused on the contribution found within the Trinity concerning unity within diversity and how that speaks into current challenges within professional chaplaincy. In truth, it must be acknowledged that there are various images and forms of unity within the Bible.

The Bible has both dualistic and paradoxical thinking. Some of us within the human family are more apt to embrace dualistic thinking. Some of us in the human family only know peace in paradoxical thinking. Each type of thinking can add hope and meaning on individual, contextual, and societal levels.

The biblical passage Mark 3:25, "And if a house is divided against itself, that house will not be able to stand" is an example of dualistic thinking. Another example is John 10:9, "I am the gate. Whoever enters by me will be saved and will come in and go out and find pasture." Both of these passages present an either/or paradigm. The house either remains united and stands or it can divide against itself and fall. One can either enter by the gate of Jesus and be saved or be snatched up by the thief who "comes only to steal and kill and destroy" (John 10:10a).

The Trinity is an example of paradoxical thinking that is not limited to the confines of the human imagination. An example of paradoxical thinking within the Bible would include 1 Cor 15:53, "For this perishable body must put on imperishability, and this mortal body must put on immortality."

The apostle Peter shares an image of unity grounded on the cornerstone of Christ. First Peter 2:4–5 reads, "Come to him, a living stone, though rejected by mortals yet chosen and precious in God's sight, and like living stones, let yourselves be built into a spiritual house, to be a holy priesthood, to offer spiritual sacrifices acceptable to God through Jesus Christ."

The previous chapter examined a unity within diversity rooted in a common confession in Christ in Johannine theology, understanding this unity as an indication of the Holy Spirit and love in action that moves beyond one's community and, with the inspiration of the Holy Spirit, seeks to include all people. These teachings echo John 15, where Jesus refers to himself as "the true vine" (John 15:1a) and recognizes the need to remain connected to the vine to bear fruit. Jesus said, "I am the vine, you are the branches. Those who abide in me and I in them bear much fruit, because apart from me you can do nothing" (John 15:5). Later, Jesus repeats the love commandment: "This is my commandment, that you love one another as I have loved you" (John 15:12).

The apostle Paul uses the image of the body of Christ and moves us towards unity within authenticity. In 1 Cor 12:14–20 he writes,

> Indeed, the body does not consist of one member but of many. If the foot would say, "Because I am not a hand, I do not belong to the body," that would not make it any less a part of the body. And if the ear would say, "Because I am not an eye, I do not belong to the body," that would not make it any less a part of the body. If the whole body were an eye, where would the hearing be? If the whole body were hearing, where would the sense of smell be? But as it is, God arranged the members in the body, each one of them as he chose. If all were a single member, where would the body be? As it is, there are many members, yet one body.

The Anglican archbishop Desmond Tutu writes, "God gives us the freedom to be authentically ourselves."[21] Later Tutu wrote, concerning the issue of power and service as it relates to community,

> Jesus tried to propagate a new paradigm of power. Power and might in this paradigm are not meant for self-aggrandizement, not meant to be lorded over others. Power and might are not for throwing our weight about, disregarding any laws and conventions we may find inconvenient. Power in this new paradigm is for

---

21. Tutu, *God Has a Dream*, 34.

service—for being compassionate, for being gentle, for being caring—for being servant to all.[22]

Practical Implications for Professional Chaplaincy

In a paradoxical way within the ministry of professional chaplaincy, the reality of pluralism and the mystery of the Trinity push those who dwell within belief systems containing an absolute truth (including the evangelical Christian professional chaplain) to live into the truth of the blessedness of all persons more faithfully, into the world as one's true mission field, and into the need to faithfully seek to be healing agents in all situations and with all people. At the same time, those who dwell within belief systems that contain an absolute truth (including the evangelical Christian professional chaplain) push those living within a pluralistic worldview to live within their own worldview more faithfully—that is, not falling into the reality of power and division within community but rather living in harmony within community, which is the original goal of pluralistic thought.

Following the contributions of the Trinity and Christian thinkers like the apostle Paul and Desmond Tutu we are led to the concept of authenticity. It is here that the connection with professional chaplaincy is strong since authenticity is an essential part of the ministry of professional chaplaincy and of every spiritual care encounter.

In practical terms this would mean large spiritual care departments would seek a vast array of professional chaplains including those working from a pluralistic worldview and those working from an absolute truth worldview. In this way, there is a role for the evangelical Christian in the ministry of professional chaplaincy. In fact, there is a *necessary* role for the evangelical Christian in the ministry of professional chaplaincy.

---

22. Tutu, *God Has a Dream*, 121.

Spiritual Discernment Questions

1. This chapter describes the differences between a pastoral care visit and a spiritual care encounter. Explain.

2. Are there times when a spiritual care encounter may shift to a pastoral care visit to better meet the needs of those being served? Explain what this might look like in real time.

3. In what ways does the evangelical Christian professional chaplain assist the profession of chaplaincy to live into its own mission and ministry more fully?

Chapter 4

Paradigm Shifts in the World of Professional Chaplaincy and a Role for Evangelical Christian Chaplains

"The harvest is plentiful, but the laborers are few..."
Luke 10:2

IN THE TWENTY-FIRST CENTURY, God is opening many opportunities for professional chaplains to be in ministry in a variety of areas. These areas include prison chaplaincy, military chaplaincy, workplace chaplaincy, first-responder chaplaincy, marketplace professional chaplaincy, professional/collegiate sports chaplaincy, hospice chaplaincy, and healthcare/hospital chaplaincy. In this chapter, I will explore the opportunities currently available and developing in the near future regarding healthcare/hospital chaplaincy.

There are four main accreditation associations for professional chaplains in the United States. These include the National Association of Catholic Chaplains (NACC), the National Association of Jewish Chaplains (NAJC), the National Association of Veterans Affairs Chaplains (NACC), and the Association of Professional Chaplains (APC). Affiliation in one of these endorsing agencies is a requirement for most employment opportunities. I will be focusing on accreditation through APC (Association of Professional Chaplains). In this way, I will be concentrating and considering a role for the evangelical Christian in the world of professional chaplaincy.

Literary Review

This literary review will examine two seismic paradigm shifts occurring within the world of professional chaplaincy. The first shift is moving from the existing idea that serving the spiritual care needs of another can impact *how* a patient gets better to a new developing understanding that serving the spiritual care needs of another can impact *if* a patient gets better. The second shift occurring in the world of professional chaplaincy revolves around the former understanding of a pluralistic worldview as a requirement to be a professional chaplain to a new perspective centering around authenticity in the practice of professional chaplaincy. Finally, with this new foundation of authenticity in practice, the question arises, What does this mean for faith traditions that hold an absolute truth? Is there a role for the evangelical Christian in the world of professional chaplaincy?

The existing understanding of the role of the professional chaplain focuses on the idea that serving the spiritual care needs of another can impact how a patient gets better. Within this traditional understanding, the professional chaplain is part of the team providing patient-centered care to the individual patient.[1] This is consistent with many of the competencies required by BCCI (Board of Chaplaincy Certification);[2] membership with the BCCI is necessary to become an affiliate of the Association of Professional Chaplains (APC). These BCCI competencies include the following:

- Section I: Integration of Theory and Practice Competencies

---

1. Wirpsa et al., "Interprofessional Models."
2. BCCI, *Competency Essay Writing Guide.*

- ITP5: "Articulate a conceptual understanding of group dynamics and organizational behavior."
- Section III: Professional Practice Skills Competencies
- PPS2: "Provide effective spiritual support that contributes to the well-being of the care recipients, their families, and staff."
- Section IV: Organizational Leadership Competencies
- OL1: "Promote the integration of spiritual care into the life and service of the institution in which one functions."
- OL2: "Establish and maintain professional and interdisciplinary relationships."[3]

Lynn Bassett builds on this team approach and the work of others in examining the role of the professional chaplain at end-of-life.[4] In this way she is building on the work and traditional understanding of professional chaplains, as do Piderman and associates, who conducted a survey at the Mayo Clinic that reported 39 percent of patients and families ranked the chaplain's intervention as very or somewhat important when making difficult medical decisions.[5] Another study examined the positive role of the professional chaplain among African American patients and families facing end-of-life decisions.[6]

Significant research has occurred on the role of the professional chaplain within palliative care and hospice services and in the process of making end-of-life decisions. These studies build upon the traditional understanding that the role of the professional chaplain affects how a patient and their family experience their overall care. A research article titled "A National Study on Chaplaincy Services and End-of Life Outcomes" suggests that chaplaincy services may play a role in increased hospice enrollment in end-of-life care services. This increased hospice enrollment often correlates to more patients fulfilling their wishes to

3. BCCI, *Competencies Rubric*, 6, 16, 26–27.
4. Bassett, "Space, Time and Shared Humanity."
5. Piderman et al., "Patient Expectations," 58.
6. Grant et al., "Chaplain's Role."

die at home. This function of the professional chaplain has then correlated to greater satisfaction rates among families who believe their spiritual needs and those of their loved ones have been valued, honored, and cared for.[7]

The new paradigm in professional chaplaincy does not deny the growing evidence that professional chaplaincy positively affects how a patient gets better; rather the new paradigm in professional chaplaincy is expanding the understanding of professional chaplaincy to also include many times *if* a patient gets better. A growing number of studies examine the role of spiritual care by studying its effects on a person's perspective on finding meaning in life, on social connectedness, and on loneliness. These studies then examine those outcomes with regard to patient recovery from physical illness and mental illness and with regard to an increase in life expectancy.

Independent studies conducted by Stanford University and the English Longitudinal Study of Aging, an ongoing British study of older adults directed by Andrew Steptoe, a psychologist and epidemiologist at University of London, found that the feeling that one's life has meaning is associated with positive health outcomes.[8] For many people, personal faith is a source of meaning. A professional chaplain has the role of seeking to bring forth whatever has given the patient, family, or staff member hope, meaning, and strength in the past. In this way, the professional chaplain assists the patient, family, or staff member to reestablish their connection with whatever has given them hope, meaning, and strength. Further, the professional chaplain must be open to whatever way that patient, family, or staff member answers the question of what gives them hope, meaning, and strength. Therefore, one of the central roles of a professional chaplain is to connect the people being served with their personal source of meaning in life. This study builds upon the work of Benedetti who discovered that a

---

7. Flannelly et al., "End of Life Outcomes."

8. Steptoe, quoted in Denworth, "Power and Purpose," paras. 1–3; see also Parker, "Meaningful Life."

patient's thoughts, attitudes, and emotions play a central role in health outcomes.[9]

Several recent studies have built upon the work of Julianne Holt-Lunstad, Timothy B. Smith, and J. Bradley Layton in their study "Social Relationships and Mortality Risk: A Meta-analytic Review," which began to investigate the health factors associated with loneliness.[10] Further investigations include studies conducted independently by the Cleveland Clinic and Harvard Medical School surrounding the effects of loneliness. Both institutions concluded that the effects of loneliness have reached epidemic levels in the United States and can be as much of a threat to a person's health as obesity.[11] A recent study on loneliness reported 36 percent of respondents feel lonely "frequently" or "almost all the time or all the time."[12]

Further, studies have indicated that loneliness can have negative health risks and these negative health risks affect a similar number of patients as those adversely affected by smoking.[13] A study conducted by the Mayo Clinic demonstrates that loneliness is linked to increased emergency department visits for chronic obstructive pulmonary disease.[14] Another study suggests a link between loneliness and a higher susceptibility to Alzheimer's disease.[15]

Clearly research has shown that loneliness is a serious problem in our world today. These findings are consistent from a Christian theological perspective. Desmond Tutu spoke into the issue of loneliness when he wrote, "God has made us in such a way that we need each other. We are made for companionship

---

9. Benedetti, "Placebo and the New Physiology."
10. Holt-Lunstad et al., "Social Relationships."
11. Gupta, "Loneliness"; Cleveland Clinic, "When You're Lonely."
12. Weissbourd et al., "Loneliness in America," para. 4.
13. Harvard Health Publishing, "Same Risk"; Frame, "Julianne-Holt"; Yeh, "Prevalence of Loneliness."
14. Marty et al., "Loneliness and ED Visits."
15. Healthy Brains, "Loneliness and Alzheimer's."

and relationship. It is not good for us to be alone."[16] Mother Teresa wrote on the importance of a compassionate presence: "There are many medicines and cures for all kinds of sick people. But unless kind hands are given in service and generous hearts are given in love, I do not think there can ever be any cure for the terrible sickness of feeling unloved."[17]

Addressing loneliness is another role of the professional chaplain. A professional chaplain has extensive training in active and empathetic listening. Further, the chaplain is a team member who has the time to provide and the role of providing pastoral presence. This pastoral presence can be as simple as holding a hand, or listening as a person or family member struggles with processing life-changing events, or providing emotional and grief support. Another way the professional chaplain provides support is to make connections with a patient's support system including family, friends, a church, synagogue, mosque, or other community members.

Meeting spiritual needs has been shown to be an important component in the recovery process for mental health patients.[18] A recent study in the United Kingdom compared the effectiveness of primary care chaplaincy (PCC) to patients receiving antidepressants. The findings of the study suggest "primary care chaplaincy (and PCC alone) is associated with similar improvements in well-being to that of antidepressants and certainly no worse. This seems to justify its use as a 'talking therapy' alternative to medication."[19]

A recent edition of *All Things Considered* on National Public Radio titled "This Ivy League Researcher Says Spirituality Is Good for Mental Health" interviewed Dr. Lisa Miller of Columbia University. When relating spirituality as a source of resilience to addiction, Dr. Miller said, "The protective benefit of personal spirituality, meaning someone who says their personal spirituality is very important, is 80% against addiction. They have 80%

16. Tutu, *God Has a Dream*, 25.
17. Teresa, *Heart of the World*, 39.
18. Gomi et al., "Spiritual Assessment."
19. Macdonald, "Primary Care Chaplaincy," 362.

decreased relative risk for the DSM diagnosis of addiction to drugs or alcohol."[20] Later in the interview Dr. Miller noted a similar relationship between personal spirituality and suicide—those who consider themselves spiritual are 82 percent less likely to commit suicide.[21]

Another study demonstrated slower HIV disease progression when the spiritual care needs of the patient are met.[22] In the article "Spirituality in HIV+ Patient Care," the authors highlight the central importance of addressing the religious and spiritual needs of persons living with a chronic illness such as HIV.[23] Another study concluded that spirituality uniquely predicts health and well-being outcomes in those with HIV/AIDS. This includes improvements in life satisfaction, functional health status, and health-related quality of life.[24]

Extensive research has been conducted demonstrating the positive impact of spiritual care with cancer patients.[25] This includes improved quality of life outcomes in patients with advanced cancer whose spiritual needs were met.[26] The study "Religious and Spiritual Support Among Advanced Cancer Patients and Associations with End-of-Life Treatment" continued to build on these findings in a multisite study of 343 patients with advanced cancer. The study revealed that patients who believed their spiritual needs had been attended to had quality of life scores at life's end that were 28 percent greater than those who did not receive spiritual care.[27]

A report from the Nurses' Health Study followed the religious practices of more than seventy-four thousand participants for sixteen years. The study reported that women who attended weekly

20. Miller, "Good for Mental Health," para. 15.
21. Miller, "Good for Mental Health," para. 40.
22. Rey, "Report."
23. Utley and Wachholtz, "Spirituality."
24. Pargament et al., "Religion and HIV."
25. National Cancer Institute, "Spirituality in Cancer Care."
26. Balboni et al., "Religiousness."
27. Balboni and Peteet, "Spirituality and Religion."

religious services had a lower mortality rate compared to those who never attended religious services.[28]

Finally, independent studies have shown that there is a range from four to fourteen years greater life expectancy for persons who believe in God.[29] Volunteerism and involvement in social organizations accounted for less than a year in increased life longevity, much lower than found in persons who hold a belief in God.[30]

In summary, many studies, all dated from the year 2000 to the present have repeatedly provided evidence-based research demonstrating a correlation between care provided by a professional chaplain and improved patient outcomes. This evidence-based research is giving increased credibility to the services provided by the professional chaplain. This evidence-based research is also spurring the growth of spiritual care departments and opportunities for professional chaplains.

The second shift occurring in the world of professional chaplaincy centers around the need for professional chaplains to serve all persons within their multicultural society. As discussed in chapter 3 in the section titled "Contributions from Professional Chaplaincy," there was a time when the working assumption requiring a pluralistic worldview for professional chaplaincy began to switch to the new working assumption requiring authenticity for professional chaplaincy.

The article "The Chaplain as an Authentic and an Ethical Presence" challenges the working assumption that professional chaplains "must always be with people where they are," an assumption that can be made within a pluralistic worldview, and advocates instead for authenticity, which drives the spiritual care encounter. It is recognized that chaplains must respect the religious practices and traditions that are not their own. The writers also question the ethical standards of attempting to authentically enter the spiritual and religious practices that are not personally lived out by the chaplain. The authors question if such a practice

28. Li et al., "Religious Service Attendance."
29. Matthews-King, "Religious People Live"; Rey, "Report."
30. Matthews-King, "Religious People Live."

may do harm to both those being served and the chaplain. Instead, the authors emphasize the need for the professional chaplain to make referrals to other professionals who can then best serve a patient's or family's needs.[31] This is consistent with the Common Code of Ethics for Chaplains, Pastoral Counselors, Pastoral Educators, and Students.[32]

Military chaplain John D. Lang, in his book *In Jesus' Name: Evangelicals and Military Chaplaincy,* highlights the importance of incarnational relationships[33] based on the authenticity of the chaplain.[34] Dr. Otis Corbitt, also a military chaplain, echoes the necessity for authenticity in the often-incarnational ministry of chaplaincy[35] and further emphasizes the reality that much of the authority of a chaplain comes from their authenticity and their moral and ethical character.[36]

This shift in thought in the world of professional chaplaincy is occurring for two reasons. The first is the witness of professional chaplains since 2004 who have served effectively as professional chaplains and do not uphold a pluralistic worldview and the Common Standards for Professional Chaplaincy mandate. The second is the realization that requiring a pluralistic worldview effectively excludes anyone of any faith tradition that holds to an absolute truth. Further, if a pluralistic worldview is needed to be an effective professional chaplain then this need itself becomes its own absolute truth.

The exclusion of anyone or any faith tradition that holds an absolute truth excludes many faith traditions from professional chaplaincy. A few examples include the Jewish believer who holds the absolute truth, "There is no other God but Yahweh"; the Catholic believer who holds the absolute truth, "Salvation is known in and through the Church"; the Muslim believer who holds the

31. Zucker et al., "Chaplain as Authentic Presence."
32. Common Code of Ethics for Chaplains.
33. Lang, *In Jesus' Name,* 155–56.
34. Lang, *In Jesus' Name,* 283, 292.
35. Corbitt, *Introduction to Chaplaincy,* 36–37.
36. Corbitt, *Introduction to Chaplaincy,* 50.

absolute truth of Mohammed's teachings and the teachings of the Koran; and the evangelical Christian believer who holds the absolute truth, "Jesus Saves."

What is a role for an evangelical Christian who might feel called to professional chaplaincy and how might the evangelical Christian navigate the process of board certification? Many if not most institutions require full-time chaplains to receive board certification. This process includes a master of divinity degree, four Clinical Pastoral Education (CPE) units, which are followed by two thousand hours of supervised practice and endorsement from the candidate's denominational endorsing agency. Upon completion of these requirements the candidate can then seek an interview with the Board of Chaplaincy Certification (BCCI) an affiliate of the Association of Professional Chaplains (APC).

During the BCCI interview the chaplaincy candidate needs to demonstrate proficiency in thirty-one competencies. At the conclusion of the interview three outcomes can happen. First, if it is agreed by the committee that the candidate demonstrated proficiency in all thirty-one competencies, the candidate then passes and is recommended for full BCCI membership and APC membership (the gold standard for spiritual care and education). A second possible outcome is the candidate is determined to have successfully demonstrated proficiency in most of the thirty-one competencies, but the committee believes there are a few proficiencies that require more work. When this occurs, a candidate has two years from the date of the first interview to apply for a "subsequent appearance." During this follow-up interview the committee will only interview the candidate on those proficiencies that were deemed to need more work in the first interview. In a third scenario the candidate demonstrates a lack of knowledge and achievement on most proficiencies, in which case it is determined by the committee that BCCI certification for the candidate cannot be recommended.

Authenticity in a chaplain's ministry is a competency located twice within the following BCCI requirements:

- Section II: Professional Identity and Conduct Competencies

- PIC2: "Articulate ways in which one's feelings, attitudes, values, and assumptions affect professional practice."
- Section III: Professional Practice Skills Competencies
- PPS1: "Establish, deepen, and conclude spiritual care relationships with sensitivity, openness, and respect."[37]

Proficiency in these competencies is necessary for three reasons. First, by becoming aware of who you are on a deep level you can then use this tool of self-awareness as a resource for providing spiritual care to patients, families, and staff. The apostle Paul wrote "for whenever I am weak then I am strong" (2 Cor 12:10b). Those who have experienced grief are often able to tap into this aspect of who they are to simply be an authentic, compassionate, non-anxious presence with another who is experiencing intense grief without having to emotionally or physically "escape" the situation. This is a practical example of how a professional chaplain can use authenticity as a healing practice in providing spiritual care. In his classic book *The Wounded Healer* Henri Nouwen explores this principle of a person's wounds transformed by God to become a vehicle of healing to others.[38]

Second, a professional chaplain needs to be self-aware enough to know when (not if) a situation or a patient's experience "sticks to you" and even gets under your skin. Everyone will eventually have this happen because we are human, and we enter each situation with our own previous experiences, feelings, and attitudes. Having a spiritual care counselor or a good team of colleagues to process these situations with when they occur is invaluable if a professional chaplain wants to have any longevity in the profession.

Third, as mentioned earlier, the role of the professional chaplain as an authentic, compassionate, non-anxious presence who can maintain rational cognitive thinking in all situations is the starting point for every patient, family, and staff encounter. If this does not occur, then the professional chaplain can be a hindrance rather than a calming, healing influence. Being a compassionate,

37. BCCI, *Competencies Rubric*, 9, 15.
38. Nouwen, *Wounded Healer*.

non-anxious presence who is able to maintain rational cognitive thinking can be an effective spiritual care encounter, and there are times when this is all that can be done. At the same time, part of the "art of chaplaincy" is using one's training and experience to assist the patient, family, or staff member receiving care to access within themselves whatever has given their life hope, meaning, and strength in the past.

The professional chaplain must be open to however that person, family, or staff member answers the question of what gives their life hope, meaning, and strength. This is consistent with BCCI requirements as well:

- Section II: Professional Identity and Conduct Competencies
- PIC4: Function in a manner that "respects the physical, emotional, cultural, and spiritual boundaries of others."[39]
- Section III: Professional Practice Skills Competencies
- PPS1: "Establish, deepen and conclude professional spiritual care relationships with sensitivity, openness, and respect."[40]
- PPS3: Provide spiritual care that respects diversity and differences in areas including but not limited to culture, gender, sexual orientation and spiritual/religious practices.[41]

In this way, spiritual care as a professional chaplain is not a time of proselytizing; rather, it is a time of *representative ministry*—a ministry of presence and walking alongside those being served.

Challenges for Evangelicals in the World of Professional Chaplaincy

In the past evangelical chaplains have often encountered hurdles and difficulties in the process of board certification and the practice of serving as a professional chaplain. The section of chapter

39. BCCI, *Competencies Rubric*, 11.
40. BCCI, *Competencies Rubric*, 15.
41. BCCI, *Competencies Rubric*, 17.

3 titled "Current Challenges Experienced by Pluralism" recorded the results of research by Dr. Michael Elmore and the experience of evangelical professional chaplains.

To further explore this reality experienced by many evangelical Christians I chose to look to Dietrich Bonhoeffer and ask the question, Would Dietrich Bonhoeffer successfully pass all thirty-one competencies and be recommended for full BCCI membership? To answer this question, I read Bonhoeffer's book *Spiritual Care* through the lens of a BCCI candidate preparing for their BCCI interview. I have served on the interview committees several times and, on my reading, Bonhoeffer would be challenged by the interview committee along two lines. First, he would be challenged because his audience for spiritual care includes his parishioners.[42] Second, Bonhoeffer suggests the role of the spiritual care provider is to assist the person receiving spiritual care in making sense of their illness or malady in the context of their Christian faith.[43] Through example and representative ministry, Bonhoeffer would have to describe and demonstrate proficiency in BCCI requirements PIC2, PIC4, PPS1, PPS3 and PPS8, which can be summarized as follows: facilitate theological/spiritual reflection for those in one's care practice.[44] Without describing and demonstrating proficiency in these five proficiencies, as a BCCI review member, I would recommend Bonhoeffer for a "subsequent appearance."

I chose to examine Bonhoeffer as a BCCI candidate because Bonhoeffer's life and contribution to the Christian faithful and to the world make it clear that not everyone may be called to serve as a professional chaplain. Second, I chose him because of his witness and the congruency between his thought and life. In this way, Bonhoeffer, for many, is a witness of an authentically lived life. Christiane Tietz emphasizes the integral connectedness of Bonhoeffer's

---

42. Bonhoeffer, *Spiritual Care*, 30–31, 37, 44, 56, 59.
43. Bonhoeffer, *Spiritual Care*, 30, 34–35, 44.
44. BCCI, *Competencies Rubric*, 9, 11, 15, 17, 22.

life, thought, and theology,[45] his embodiment of one who "trie[s] to preserve the relationship between faith, theology and life."[46]

Dietrich Bonhoeffer (1906–45) was born in Breslau, Germany. At age twenty-five he was ordained in the evangelical church. Bonhoeffer was a firm opponent of Hitler's philosophy and sought to organize the Protestant church to reject Nazi ideology thus assisting and serving in a breakaway movement, the Confessing Church. Despite opportunities to escape to the United States during World War II, Bonhoeffer chose to return to Germany from his travels providing lectures throughout the world and remained there to share the struggles of his fellow countrymen. He believed he needed to have the courage to live what he taught and preached. In April 1943, Bonhoeffer was arrested by the Nazis and he spent the rest of his life in a Nazi prison camp until he was executed by hanging on April 8, 1945.[47]

Recognizing that Bonhoeffer would have need to improve in certain areas if he had chosen to pursue BCCI recommendation and a ministry as a professional chaplain does not mean that Bonhoeffer does not have something to teach those who are in the world of professional chaplaincy. Specifically, Bonhoeffer has much to teach us in our understanding and practice of PPS8: Facilitate theological/spiritual reflection for those in one's care practice.[48] Bonhoeffer prods us to recognize that there are times when a patient, family or staff member may be best served by a professional chaplain who resides in their own faith tradition. One example would be a Catholic patient who would have their spiritual care needs met best by a priest who can perform an Anointing of the Sick.

---

45. Tietz, *Theologian of Resistance*, vii.
46. Tietz, *Theologian of Resistance*, 118.
47. Sherman, "Dietrich Bonhoeffer."
48. BCCI, *Competencies Rubric*, 22.

A Role for the Evangelical in the World of Professional Chaplaincy

I remember one specific situation in the hospital. Often, I am called to come to the bedside of a patient to pray. This has been a meaningful spiritual encounter that I have provided as a professional chaplain in all situations but this one. In this situation, there was a woman who had been on a breathing machine for several days and was to be taken off the breathing machine because her condition had improved. I was called because the patient had requested prayer before this medical procedure took place. This is not uncommon, and I had been called into this type of situation several times.

When I arrived, I spoke with the registered nurse and she said the patient was very agitated. I learned that there was concern that the patient may not be able to be removed from the breathing machine due to her agitation and her refusal to have the breathing machine removed without having prayer. After I introduced myself, the patient anxiously tried to write something on a piece of paper. After some effort, I realized the patient was asking me if I prayed in tongues. I gave my answer to her question, referring to 1 Cor 12 where the apostle Paul speaks of various gifts. I explained to the patient that while I have been blessed with some gifts and knew other believers who had received this gift, I had not personally received the gift of speaking in tongues at this point in my life. The patient then made it clear that she wanted nothing to do with me and kicked me out of the room.

Fortunately, I work with a female professional chaplain staff member who has the gift of speaking in tongues. She was working that day and I alerted her to the situation. She was able to arrive in a few minutes and serve the spiritual care needs of the patient. The patient was taken off the breathing machine and was later able to explain to Lynn, my fellow staff member, why she felt a need to pray in tongues before being taken off the breathing machine, further deepening the spiritual care healing that could be provided to her.

An example like the one above challenges the world of professional chaplaincy in two ways: First, there is the reality that a pluralistic worldview of a professional chaplain followed by an inauthentic prayer by the chaplain would not have best served the spiritual care needs of this patient. In a situation such as this, the professional chaplain would need to locate a local clergyperson who could meet the spiritual care needs of the patient, something that could have been very difficult in a time-sensitive case such as this. Second, this type of situation highlights the need for spiritual care departments to seek a variety of perspectives and faith traditions within their department rather than relying on chaplains who have a pluralistic worldview.

In his book *The Myth of the Dying Church* Glenn T. Stanton examines an Indiana University / Harvard research study, which found that from 1972 to 2016 the number of evangelicals in the United States grew from 18 percent of the population in 1972 to 28 percent of the population.[49] This study points to the reality that many people in the United States need to pray "in Jesus' name" to best meet their spiritual care needs. There are times, as Bonhoeffer taught, that assisting the person receiving spiritual care in making sense of their illness or malady in the context of their Christian faith is the best practice that the professional chaplain can provide. Therefore, it would seem consistent and obvious that having evangelical professional chaplains on staff would serve as an asset to a spiritual care department and to those they serve.

There have been times when I have heard evangelical Christians considering professional chaplaincy as a ministry express concerns that they would need to compromise their beliefs or that they might be denied the opportunity to serve as a professional chaplain because of their beliefs. One response to this concern is the recognition that every chaplain must be endorsed by their denominational endorsing agency and cannot be required by their position as a professional chaplain to function in a manner outside the rules and regulations of the denomination of which they are a member.

---

49. Stanton, *Myth of the Dying Church*, 17.

Further, free speech and religious liberty eventually carried the day in the case of the chaplain Gordon Klingenschmitt. In 2007 Congress rebuked the Navy by rescinding SECNAVINST 1730.7C in a conference report, thus restoring liberty to all military chaplains to pray freely, while in uniform or not, and gave them the freedom to pray seven days a week.[50] This meant that going forward all chaplains, regardless of their religion or denominational status, can pray authentically, including those chaplains who pray "in Jesus' name." This conference report to the 2007 Defense Authorization Act was signed by President George W. Bush who ordered the Navy to comply.[51]

Several recent Supreme Court decisions have ruled in favor of religious liberties. These rulings include the 2014 case of *Burwell v. Hobby Lobby*, which ruled that a private business cannot be forced to practice in ways that fall outside of their religious beliefs.[52] The 2018 case *Masterpiece Cakeshop v. Colorado Civil Rights Commission* ruled that a private citizen cannot be forced to work and function in ways outside of their personal religious conviction.[53] The 2020 case *Little Sisters of the Poor v. Pennsylvania*[54] and the 2021 case *Fulton v. City of Philadelphia*[55] both upheld the rights of religiously founded institutions to act and function in ways consistent with their religious beliefs and values. The 2022 case *Kennedy vs. Bremerton School District* acknowledged an individual's right to prayer and religious expression in a public setting as guaranteed by the First Amendment.[56] All these Supreme Court rulings defend and advocate for forms of authenticity in practice for those who hold and live by religious principles.

---

50. Department of the Navy, "SECNAVINST 1730.7D N097."
51. See PrayInJesusName.org.
52. Oyez, "Burwell v. Hobby Lobby Stores."
53. Oyez, "Masterpiece v. Colorado."
54. Oyez, "Little Sisters v. Pennsylvania."
55. Oyez, "Fulton v. Philadelphia."
56. Oyez, "Kennedy v. Bremerton."

A New Mission Field

As the twenty-first century reaches its third decade, God is creating a new mission field, and the various roles performed by professional chaplains is one way God is sharing the good news of Jesus Christ to communities within the United States and throughout the world. A recent study conducted by Gallup for the Chaplaincy Innovation Lab at Brandeis University reported that "one in four Americans have interacted with a chaplain at some point in their lives."[57] The article revealed that most people reported the interaction with the chaplain was valuable to them—44 percent called it very valuable and 32 percent, moderately valuable. Another 17 percent said the encounter was only a little valuable, while 7 percent described it as not valuable at all.[58]

The Gallup study provides empirical evidence for what is intuitively known and experienced. Professional chaplains are often serving people from various faith perspectives, including people with no faith perspective. The chaplain encounter "often connects faith leaders with non-religious people—constituting 42% of those who have interacted with a chaplain."[59] Taken together, it is evident that many times it is the professional chaplain in representative ministry who serves as the hands and feet of the gospel. Further, since 76 percent of those served by a chaplain reported the encounter to be valuable or moderately valuable one can reasonably assume that many of these chaplain encounters occurred between the chaplain and nonreligious persons and often these encounters were experienced as either very valuable or moderately valuable.

Within this new mission field, the structure and form of sharing the gospel is different from what may have been considered the norm. Often the sharing of the good news of Jesus Christ is understood to occur in the church and through the form of proclamation. This form of proclamation will continue to bear fruit for the kingdom of God. However, in the postmodern world we live

---

57. Saad, "One in Four Americans," para. 1.
58. Saad, "One in Four Americans," para. 17.
59. Saad, "One in Four Americans," para. 20.

in today, in the United States, many would never enter a church. Therefore, these people would not be able to hear the good news proclaimed.

God in God's love and wisdom is creating ways to reach the unchurched by going to where people reside. This is not the first time in Christian history where God has sent the faithful to people to share the good news and transform the world of their day. A few examples include Francis of Assisi (1181–1226), John Wesley (1703–91), Florence Nightingale (1820–1910), Aimee Elizabeth Semple McPherson (1890–1944) and Mother Teresa (1910–97). In a similar way, professional chaplaincy takes place outside of the church walls to where people live, into their daily lives and activities.

In this way, the form of sharing the good news of Jesus Christ changes from a proclamation of the word to representative ministry. When serving in a pastoral role, conversion to Jesus and salvation in Christ is essential to what is done. As a professional chaplain, proselytizing and seeking conversion is inappropriate and unacceptable. Rather, representation and being an authentic living presence of comfort and hope is essential and is the appropriate form of ministry for the professional chaplain.

A representative form of ministry is encapsulated in Matt 25:34–45, where Jesus teaches a series of lessons and summarizes the teaching saying, "I tell you, whatever you did for one of the least of these brothers and sisters of mine, you did it for me" (Matt 25:40). Francis of Assisi reflected this form of teaching when he said, "Preach the gospel at all times and if all else fails use words."[60]

At the same time, because we live in a pluralistic culture and the site of ministry is where people live, the professional chaplain often encounters and serves people who are non-Christian. These encounters begin and end in the same way—with a compassionate, authentic presence who can maintain rational cognitive thinking when often the people involved cannot. Many times, in the hospital setting, these patients and families seem surprised that a Christian chaplain can be an authentic person of comfort and

---

60. This phrase is generally attributed to St. Francis of Assisi.

compassion and is willing to meet them "as they are" and assist them in drawing forth in themselves whatever has given their life hope, meaning, and strength.

One encounter of mine is representative of several similar encounters in ministry with non-Christian patients and families. I was called to a patient's room because the patient's health was declining. As I approached the room the patient was intubated, on life-support, and non-responsive. I noticed a woman sitting in the corner of the room and, as is my custom, I entered the room and introduced myself. The woman was polite and explained to me that she and her husband were Hindu. I asked if it was okay for me to sit down. She agreed and with little to no prompting she launched into telling me her life story.

She spoke about meeting her husband and moving from India to the United States due to her husband's work. She shared stories of their family and their life together. Having a compassionate presence appeared to comfort her, someone who honored the telling of her life story seemed meaningful and empowering. Before I left, I asked her if I could do anything else. She informed me that as Hindus they believed all prayers went to God. She then asked me if I would pray to God for her husband. I told her I would be honored. I placed my hand on the patient and prayed to God thanking God for the patient and who he is, asking for God's comfort for all who love him, and asking for God's special blessing to be upon him. The patient's wife watched me intently and at the prayer's conclusion thanked me emphatically.

When I left the room (the visit took about forty-five minutes), I was approached by two nurses who were shocked that I was able to talk to the wife of the patient. They informed me that they did not know she spoke English and that every time someone had spoken to the family the man present would speak on behalf of the family. As I have reflected upon this encounter, I have realized that I could have traveled the world and would never have had an experience like this due to cultural reasons. I would have never been able to share the gospel to this woman and reveal to her something different from what she may have expected or experienced before. As a professional hospital chaplain, I was blessed to meet this woman in a critical moment in her life and be her chaplain as well as a channel of God's peace in the midst of life's most difficult challenge.

The hospital setting is a new mission field. During the first fourteen years of my ministry, I served as a local church pastor. In this time, I spent *most* of my time with Christian people, living with and encouraging one another. Often, we spent time developing ministries in an effort to move beyond the local church and reach out to unchurched people within our communities.

Working as a hospital chaplain for the past seventeen-plus years, I spend *most* of my time with unchurched people. Many times, this is due to circumstances beyond the patient's or family's control, usually a decline in health and an inability to get to church. Other times people may not have a current church family or have not been to church for a long, long time. The stories vary; however, the compassionate, authentic presence of a professional chaplain often leads to discussions of faith because faith at some point has given their lives hope, meaning, and strength.

Listening to a person's life story and then holding hands and praying with a patient or family who has not prayed for a long time can be especially meaningful. Scripture tells us "that whenever two or more are gathered in my name there I am among them" (Matt 18:20). Many, many times during these encounters the experience is the same. As we hold hands and pray, the spirit of God is strong, and at the prayer's conclusion, the patient or family members seem to have a look of peace, comfort, and wonder. I have come to believe that during these times the truth of Scripture has been confirmed once again—for to their great surprise God has met them in that moment! God has made his presence known and has rejoined their journey as if no time had passed between prayers, for God has been loving them always. I do not believe that these encounters are an end for those patients and families; rather I believe that those encounters often lead to a renewed relationship with God.

One visit that represents many sticks in my mind. I received a patient request for a chaplain visit. Upon entry, I met a man lying on his side. He immediately sat up and seemed to welcome a chaplain visit. I asked if I could take a seat and he agreed. He began (I will call him Todd) by telling me that he "almost died." I asked him what that meant, and he dove into telling me his life story. He told me that he had "lived on Mountain Dew and cigarettes," which led to him being rushed into the emergency department and spending a few days "on a vent" and in the ICU. "I almost died," he repeated. I continued to provide empathetic listening and learned that he had been married for many years and "it was just the two of us." I also learned that he found much purpose in being a hard worker, even to the point of returning to work for several years to deliver pizzas after he officially retired. This helped me understand his comment that he had lived on Mountain Dew and cigarettes. I learned that he was nearly seventy and he and his wife had recently decided to both retire. This had occurred a few months ago, which meant that he had gone from a very active life to a very sedentary life. It also meant he had received multiple IVs while in the ICU; according to him, the doctor had informed him he would need to switch from Mountain Dew to water.

As the conversation continued, Todd informed me that he had not been to church for a long time. (I remember it kind of felt like a confession.) At the same time, he asked me if I would say a prayer for him and his wife. I agreed. I held his hand, closed my eyes (which is my custom), and prayed. The spirit felt very strong in the room. When I finished the prayer, I looked at Todd and he had tears streaming down his face. I asked him, "What does that mean?" He replied, "It was like I was eight years old." I probed further what that meant, and he explained that his grandmother would take him and his brothers and sisters to church on Sunday mornings, to "a little white church." I learned that being taken to church by his grandmother was the last time he had attended church. Yet, the ember of faith had been with him all his life. In the moment of our prayer together God had breathed on that ember and Todd was changed. He kept thanking me for the visit and the prayer. I was confident Todd would be talking to God in prayer in the future and that this encounter had a lasting impression on his life.

The direction of the ministry of the professional chaplain is to go to where the people reside and live. In her book *God in Captivity: The Rise of Faith-Based Prison Ministries in the Age of Mass Incarceration*, Tanya Erzen takes a deep dive into the realities in today's prison system in the United States. Erzen, who has worked inside prisons, simply gives a truthful picture of the reality of today's prison system. She cites truth, revealing that the United States represents 5 percent of the world's population and has 25 percent of the world's prisoners[61] and one-third of the world's female prisoners.[62] Erzen reports that one in nine of these individuals serving time in prisons, including those convicted as juveniles, are serving life sentences.[63] Erzen reports the disparities in race and incarceration, highlighting that "Black Americans are incarcerated five times more than whites, and Latinos are nearly twice as likely to be incinerated as whites."[64] Finally, Erzen examines the reality that as states determined to no longer provide funding for rehabilitation functions in prisons, faith-based ministries have stepped in to try and fill the gap.[65]

Erzen makes clear that her book is not written to examine the reasons behind these staggering realities within the prison system (some might say *prison industry*) in the United States and acknowledges that examining the reasons behind these realities is important and necessary work. Rather, she begs the question, Why are the faith-based ministries predominately evangelical?[66] Finally, she simply looks at the differences between a prison system based on a warehouse mentality and a system based on a rehabilitation mentality and acknowledges the unmistakable changes within the

61. Erzen, *God in Captivity*, 7.
62. Erzen, *God in Captivity*, 8.
63. Erzen, *God in Captivity*, 7.
64. Erzen, *God in Captivity*, 7.
65. Erzen, *God in Captivity*, 15.
66. Erzen, *God in Captivity*, 15.

lives of individual prisoners and prison facilities as a whole due to faith-based ministries.

Faith-based ministries are primarily evangelical because these ministries are rooted in a Pauline theology of blessed createdness, redemption, and new life by faith in Christ. Pauline theology is woven together with intense personal experience of the divine because that is Paul's own Damascus-road experience (Acts 9:1–20). Therefore, Paul's theology is grounded in God's grace, given as a gift and received through faith that is for all (Rom 1:16–17). Paul understands the centrality of Jesus and the need to confess that Jesus is Lord (Rom 10:9–10). Paul emphasizes time and time again the new life in Christ experienced by the believer. Romans 6:3–4, 2 Cor 5:14–21, and Eph 4:20–24 provide a non-exhaustive list of Bible passages. Finally, Paul is convinced that nothing can separate us from the love of God in Jesus Christ (Rom 8:31–39).

Because of Pauline theology evangelical Christians are unable and unwilling to see fellow human beings as worthless, irrelevant, or unredeemable. For this reason, evangelicals are unwilling and unable to see the current prison system in the United States through a warehouse model, even if these individuals have committed such heinous crimes they are serving life sentences. Evangelicals continue to see value and the possibility of God's love to enter the hearts of all people thus providing new life and freedom in Christ (Gal 5:1). Further these individuals can experience and enjoy the fruits of the Spirit (Gal 5:22–26) wherever they reside and live. This occurs because they are gifts from God and not given from any human power or authority. Fruits of the Spirit are experienced and demonstrated even in a prison where an individual may live the remainder of their earthly days.

God is creating avenues for God's people to go to the people, and professional chaplaincy is a form that God is creating for this purpose. The evangelical has an important and necessary role to play in this new mission field. The movement of professional chaplaincy for the faithful to go to where the people are is a valid and consistent biblical witness (Mark 16:15). There will continue to be a cost paid by those evangelicals called to the mission field of professional chaplaincy (John 15:20; 2 Tim 3:12); however, it is less than it was for those who traveled the path before—those trailblazers who assisted in changing the requirement for professional chaplaincy from pluralism to authenticity in personhood and practice. Finally, one more gift is from Dietrich Bonhoeffer who recognizes the potential power of authenticity and representative ministry writing, "The silent deed may lead to an ingenious proclamation."[67]

Summary

In conclusion, this literary review has examined two seismic paradigm shifts that are occurring in the world of professional chaplaincy. The first paradigm shift is the understanding that professional chaplaincy and serving the spiritual needs of another cannot only impact how a patient gets better but also includes if a patient gets better. The second paradigm shift that is occurring in the world of professional chaplaincy is the move from understanding a pluralistic worldview as being a requirement to be an effective professional chaplain to a new understanding of the importance of authenticity in practice and character as being a requirement to being an effective professional chaplain.

This movement from pluralism to authenticity opens new possibilities for any person or faith tradition that holds to an absolute truth. These two paradigm shifts taken together will open many opportunities for all persons who feel drawn to work as a professional chaplain. This includes a role for the evangelical Christian who may feel called to ministry as a professional chaplain. Authenticity means that evangelical chaplains do not need to compromise who they are or be denied the opportunity to serve as a professional chaplain. Instead, God is creating a path for the evangelical Christian, rooted in authenticity and representative ministry, to take a role within the ministry of professional chaplaincy.

---

67. Bonhoeffer, *Spiritual Care*, 51.

Spiritual Discernment Questions

1. What are the two seismic paradigm shifts that are occurring within the world of professional chaplaincy?

2. Professional chaplaincy takes place in many different areas. If you are considering professional chaplaincy as a ministry, what setting do you feel drawn too? Why?

3. This handbook cites several Supreme Court decisions that support authenticity in the believer and freedom to express one's firmly held beliefs. How might these Supreme Court decisions impact evangelical Christians in their careers and work settings?

4. How might evangelical Christian professional chaplains taking their place within their ministry and influence other evangelical Christians, in whatever career path they have taken, to live out their faith boldly and faithfully in their career and work setting? Can this be considered a form of evangelism?

Chapter 5

Living in the Mystery and Experiencing the Divine

"Now faith is the assurance of things hoped for, the conviction of things not seen."

HEBREWS 11:1

THIS CHAPTER WILL EXPLORE questions that arise from Clinical Pastoral Education (CPE). During CPE students are challenged to examine their thinking on situations that are difficult to understand, such as, suffering, life, death, and what happens after death. This chapter will examine these issues, taking into consideration my seventeen-plus years as a hospital chaplain whose primary assignment has been specializing as a crisis chaplain in an emergency department that includes all forms of trauma. My chaplaincy ministry has also included serving a thirty-two bed intensive care unit designated for COVID+ patients during the recent pandemic. During these seventeen-plus years, I have also had extensive experience within palliative care and hospice ministry.

Over the years of my ministry, there have been several situations that cannot be explained. Doctors and medical science have not been able to explain the outcome of what happened or what was experienced by a patient, their loved ones, and staff. I will share one of those experiences that I have titled "Green Sweater Grandma." This was an extremely rare occasion and in no way diminishes prayers prayed in situations that ultimately ended in the death of a patient. This will be explored in greater detail later in this chapter.

This situation began in the emergency department, as a patient was being taken by life flight to the hospital. Upon arrival I learned that the patient had been with friends in a part of a national park after hours and had fallen down a ravine. In their haste the friends of the patient ran to get help but were then unable to specifically identify where they were in the park. This led to a nearly two-day search and rescue operation until the patient (a twenty-year-old young man) was located at the bottom of the ravine. It was late fall and cold and he was found in a small creek of water. Luckily, his face was not in the water, and he did not drown. The situation was very critical. The patient was intubated and put on a breathing machine and moved to an intensive care unit. The patient's body temperature was very low, and the medical team was working to raise his body temperature.

I met his mother, father, and grandma upon arrival. They seemed anxious, exhausted (as the patient had been missing for nearly two days), relieved that he had been found, and very concerned about his condition. I escorted the family to the intensive care unit and at an appropriate time we gathered at the bedside. We stood together and I asked if the family would like prayer. At this point the patient's green sweatered grandma grabbed my hand with her right hand and she placed her left hand on the patient, and then began to pray in a way I had never heard before. I had been taught to pray with all your heart in a respectful and polite way, lifting your requests to God. Green sweater grandma prayed in a direct and powerful way that seemed like she was telling God what to do, not asking. At the end of her prayer, I simply said "amen." I remember the spirit of God felt very powerful and present in that space.

The next few weeks were long and difficult. The patient's condition remained very critical, and it even deteriorated. Originally, the mother, father, and green sweater grandma all stayed twenty-four/seven at the hospital. I continued to check in on the family and provide support; I listened as they updated me on the patient's condition and on occasion joined at the bedside for prayer. After a week or so the parents of the patient needed to return to work. This was very difficult for them. Green-sweatered grandma remained. In fact, for weeks, she never left the hospital, and medical staff became concerned for her health and well-being.

One day I began another shift at the hospital and as is my custom made my rounds in the intensive care units. I had been away for a few days. When I approached this young man's room, the room was empty. My heart sank, and I quickly went to a computer, thinking the patient had died. I knew that the family had spoken with the medical team on more than one occasion to discuss goals of care and that removing the patient from life-support and providing him with comfort care had been discussed.

When I pulled up his chart, I was surprised to see that he had been moved to a step-down unit. I felt a need to see things for myself, so I went to the room. I will never forget walking into the room and seeing the patient sitting up in bed, wearing a John Deer hat backwards, smiling, and talking to friends. I introduced myself and told him that I knew he did not know me and that I had been present when he arrived at the hospital. I told him that I had been checking in on him and that his grandma (who was sitting in a chair in the corner of the room, still wearing that green sweater) had prayed for him many times. He replied, "Oh, I know! My grandma. She's a pray-er!" I glanced at grandma and noticed a quiet smile.

Medically, there was no answer for what occurred, for the patient's recovery. Further, the level of recovery, with the patient alert and verbal, seemed beyond any reasonable hope. Yet, it had happened. In the end, that is all that can be said. How each person interprets what happened can vary. But no one can claim that it did not happen.

Many times, a professional chaplain sits with patients, families, and friends in times of suffering. During these times the professional chaplain is a non-anxious, compassionate presence. For many, introducing oneself as "a chaplain" encourages the patient, family, and friends to access their Christian faith as a means of hope, meaning, and strength. In this way, the chaplain's presence in representative ministry is a reminder of Jesus' promise "I am with you always, to the end of the age" (Matt 28: 20b).

In other situations, the professional Christian chaplain may have a situation where it is appropriate to share one's faith perspective for the benefit of the patient, family, and friends, reminding a group of Christian believers of the truth that God is with us; that God did not make this happen; that God will give us what we need to live through what we experience, for God is a God of life and resurrection. Turning to God in prayer—or for some reading the "Footprints" poem—can bring a sense of peace, healing, and strength.[1] In other situations, the professional chaplain may simply sit with a patient or family and friends in their suffering as a representative of faith who is willing to journey beside them in their suffering.

Serving during the COVID pandemic brought healthcare workers in touch with death on a scale unimagined in twenty-first-century healthcare. One sixteen-bed intensive-care unit in the hospital treated thousands of COVID+ patients, and while most lived, 275 of these patients died by Easter 2022. My book *A Chaplain's Perspective on the 2020–2021 Pandemic: Tragedy, Resilience, Hope* describes a professional chaplain's journey through this experience.

Serving others during times of death is very challenging. A normal human response to death is, Why do some people live and get better, and others die? Often the professional chaplain assists people to move beyond this question in the context of their faith perspective and worldview. It is not the place of the professional chaplain to proselytize during these moments. Rather, the professional chaplain assists persons to draw upon what has given their lives hope, meaning, and strength. Following this train of thought,

---

1. The poem is attributed to Mary Stevenson, Margaret Fishback Powers, and Carolyn Joyce Carty.

when working with a Christian family and loved ones, it is not only appropriate but is "best practice" to share words of grace and truth rooted in the Bible and one's faith tradition, which can mean praying in Jesus' name when this is the language and prayer form of those being served.

The Mystery of Death: "Therefore, since we are surrounded by so great a cloud of witnesses . . ." (Heb 12:1)

What happens after death? This is an eternal question and a reality a professional chaplain is often called into. It is, therefore, important for each professional chaplain to explore their own beliefs in order to then be able to be authentically present with others.

In my own experience as a local pastor and professional chaplain I have had many encounters with persons who have experienced a near-death experience. The frequency of these encounters was something I discussed with my peers during CPE. One of my fellow residents told me that people tell me their experience because they "know I will believe them."

I sense this is true because the first person who told me about their near-death experience was my mother. She had Guillain-Barré syndrome. She was in an intensive unit for six and half weeks, on a breathing machine, on a trach, and paralyzed from the disease. I was present when the trach was removed, and the experience poured out of her. Her near-death experience occurred on the morning of her fifty-sixth birthday, and, due to her condition, she hadn't been able to speak about the experience for weeks. We celebrated my mother's eighty-fifth birthday on January 1, 2024.

I have never asked anyone if they have had a near-death experience, yet to date, forty-six persons have shared their experience with me. Being with others and listening during these holy times has become part of my ministry. I often wonder what healing opportunities may be missed if chaplains who *believe* do not take their place among the ranks of professional chaplains. Often the individual will say, "I do not know why I am still here," and I always reply in the same way, "Maybe there is someone who needs to hear your story." Considering this, one must wonder how many missed opportunities for the growth of God's kingdom may occur if those who believe in the possibility of heaven are not present to hear, affirm, and encourage the retelling of personal near-death experiences. God might be doing amazing things that need to be shared for the growing of the kingdom of God and the benefit of others, and the professional Christian chaplain might have an important role to play within its telling.

Martin Luther King Jr. provides an important structure when examining the relationship of science and religion. This structure continues to provide wisdom as scientific research and religious thought have converged on the phenomena of near-death experiences. Rev. King wrote these words concerning the relationship between science and religion in a sermon titled "A Tough Mind and a Tender Heart":

> Science investigates; religion interprets. Science gives man knowledge and power; religion gives man wisdom which is control. Science deals mainly with facts; religion deals mainly with values. The two are not rivals. They are complimentary. Science keeps religion from sinking into the valley of crippling irrationalism and paralyzing obscurantism. Religion prevents science from falling into the marsh of obsolete materialism and moral nihilism.[2]

People who examine near-death experiences (NDEs) often fall into two different camps. One camp follows the seminal work of Raymond Moody, *Life after Life*, and proclaims NDEs as "proof" of life after life. Another camp seeks to dismiss NDEs as chemical reactions that continue to occur in the brain for a short period of time after death. Therefore, NDEs can be simply dismissed.

In this chapter, I am taking the position that neither camp is correct. From a Christian faith perspective there will always be some form of mystery when it comes to death. From a biblical perspective that is the definition of faith (Heb 11:1). In this way, NDEs

2. King, *Strength to Love*, 3–4.

may serve as a "blessed assurance" of faith while remaining outside of the realm of proof from a scientific perspective. Former registered hospice nurse Trudy Harris takes the position that NDEs are a blessed assurance in the book *Glimpses of Heaven: True Stories of Hope and Peace at the End of Life's Journey*.[3]

The wisdom from King addresses those who seek to dismiss NDEs by reminding science not to enter into the *why* question. Why do people across cultures and throughout history recount similar experiences? This is not an appropriate scientific question.

A near-death experience is "an experience, usually deeply felt and transformative, of a person near death: often, specifically, one which the person later reports had been the occasion of, variously, a feeling of out-of-body awareness, a blissful vision of an afterlife, etc."[4]

The frequency of NDEs makes the dismissal of NDEs both unsatisfactory and unscientific. One study reports a range of 10–20 percent of patients who have come close to death have experienced an NDE.[5] A more recent study suggests 23 percent of critically ill patients have experienced an NDE.[6] A recent article in *Discover Magazine* titled "Can Science Explain Near Death Experiences?" reports nine million people in the United States have experienced an NDE.[7]

Historically, NDEs have been reported throughout the ages. Plato writes of the experience of Socrates.[8] Within a biblical framework there is Stephen (Acts 7:55–56) and the apostle Paul (2 Cor 12:1–5).

Michael Fuller, in his article "Did St. Jerome: Have a Near-Death Experience?," uses modern analysis of NDEs to examine St. Jerome's recounting of a vision. He concludes, "It seems that St.

3. Harris, *Glimpses of Heaven*.
4. *Webster's New World College Dictionary*, 4th ed., s.v. "near-death experience."
5. Greyson, "Near-Death Experiences."
6. Cant et al., "Divided Self," para. 1.
7. Orlando, "Can Science Explain?," para. 1.
8. Langness, "Plato on Near-Death Experiences," paras. 4–5.

Jerome's vision on his *Letter 22* may be considered to be part of the ancient literature describing such experiences."[9]

Several books from a vast array of backgrounds and professionals have been published on this topic. These books include Mary C. Neal's book *To Heaven and Back: A Doctor's Extraordinary Account of Her Death, Heaven, Angels, and Life Again.* Mary Neal is an orthopaedic surgeon who was kayaking in Chile when she experienced an NDE.[10] In another example, Don Piper writes of his experience in his book *90 Minutes in Heaven: A True Story of Death and Life.* Don Piper is an ordained minister and was involved in a terrible car accident. He was pronounced dead by EMTs on the scene. He also recounts the incredible power of prayer that took place at the accident scene.[11] Christy Wilson Beam, a North Texas mother writes, in her book *Miracles from Heaven: A Little Girl and Her Amazing Story of Healing,* of the experience of her nine-year-old daughter Annabel.[12] Eben Alexander is an academic neurosurgeon. As a "highly trained neurosurgeon" he once believed that NDEs were nothing more than fantasies produced by brains under extreme stress. This changed when Eben experienced his own NDE. He writes of this experience in his book *Proof of Heaven: A Neurosurgeon's Journey into the Afterlife.*[13]

These books and those like them do not suggest that NDEs prove the existence of heaven. However, they serve as a growing resource of experiences across cultures, race, age, and religions that exclaim that something happens in NDEs. Something happens that fundamentally changes the individual and, often, those privileged to know them. For those who have experienced an NDE the common theme is simply that "it was real." To discount all these experiences would be unscientific and dishonest. Therefore, we are left with simply the NDE accounts themselves and each individuals wrestling with the meaning of it all.

9. Fuller, "St. Jerome."
10. Neal, *Heaven and Back*, 67–74.
11. Piper, *90 Minutes*, 37–44.
12. Beam, *Miracles from Heaven.*
13. Alexander, *Proof of Heaven*, 7–10.

In his book *My Descent into Death: A Second Chance at Life*, Howard Strom describes his NDE as extremely distressing. A studio art professor, Storm experienced an NDE while traveling with students in Paris; he recalls descending to hell, demons, and the absolute emptiness of feeling completely alone and helpless. This changed when he responded to a voice and impulse to pray to God.[14]

Storm allows us to explore the reality that not all persons who experience an NDE experience a positive experience. It is very difficult to know exactly how often this occurs since many persons who experience an NDE talk about the difficulty of finding the right words and the fear that they will not be believed or may even be ridiculed. This can make it difficult for them to share their experiences. It is logical to think that these feelings would be heightened with a person who experienced a distressing NDE. Susan Blackmore, in her book *Consciousness: An Introduction*, classifies as many as 15 percent of NDEs as negative experiences.[15]

In my own experience I have had forty-six persons tell me of their NDEs. One of these persons told me of his distressing NDE experience. Storm speaks into this and the need for a nonjudgmental listener—in other words, the need for a professional chaplain, since being a nonjudgmental listener is a fundamental service that the professional chaplain provides. Storm writes,

> Based on the number of people who have told me about their negative experiences, it appears that these are not uncommon, and it is highly unlikely that anyone will ever hear about them. Since people who had Near-Death Experiences need to process the information, and the best way for them to process it is by telling it to a nonjudgmental listener, there is a need for people in the helping professions, such as clergy, psychologists, doctors, and psychiatrists, to encourage people to share their stories without being judged or ridiculed.[16]

14. Storm, *Descent into Death*, 10–23.
15. Blackmore, *Consciousness*, 362.
16. Storm, *My Descent into Death*, 95.

Experiencing the Divine

I conclude this chapter with another bedside encounter in the hospital. Earlier I wrote about the green sweater grandma and her prayer for her grandson. In that situation a physical healing occurred that was beyond anyone's explanation. Recognizing this encounter, it must be stated that in most cases at the bedside when prayers are spoken for healing and their loved ones lift up the "groaning of their hearts" (Rom 8:26) the patient ultimately dies. I want to share an encounter from the bedside that I call "Two Hugs."

I was called by a nurse from the neurological intensive care unit with the request for a chaplain. Before entering the patient's room, the nurse and I spoke, and I was informed of the situation. I learned the patient, a woman in her late sixties, had experienced a "catastrophic" hemorrhagic stroke a few days earlier. She had been completely unresponsive and was going to die. The nurse explained that the neurological team believed she was too unstable to perform brain death testing since the life support she was on would have to be lowered; they believed once that occurred, she would die. The medical team wanted to give the family the opportunity to be in the room with the patient when life support was removed if they desired.

With this knowledge, I entered the room and met a man (I will call him Bob) who seemed anxious; he was pacing. I introduced myself and learned that the man was the son of the patient. He welcomed the chaplain's support and explained he was alone. I asked if I could get him a chair, which he declined, and then asked if it would be okay if I sat, to which he said, "That would be fine." I placed the chair at the foot of the bed and sat down, allowing space for him to continue pacing. I was trying to bring a calming presence.

During the next twenty minutes Bob would occasionally share something about his mom, though, at times we would be together for minutes in silence. I learned from Bob that the patient's husband died a few years before and that it had been very hard for her. I asked Bob how many children she had, and he told me he had a sister who lived out of town. The sister had been there the previous night. At that time, they had decided to both say their last goodbye; therefore, she would not be returning. He explained during the night he changed his mind and felt he needed to return and be present when his mom was taken off life-support. I determined this was why he was now in the room alone. He then paused and said, "Actually there were three of us." Bob then explained that he had a younger sister named Rose who died when she was seven.

The nurse and the respiratory therapist entered. We shared in prayer at the bedside over the patient upon Bob's request. The patient was then taken off life support. The room was still.

The nurse, Bob, and I stood in silence. Bob was holding his mother's left hand and crying. Then without explanation the patient very slowly moved her right arm up. She then seemed to circle her arm around and slowly lowered her arm down. She then did it a second time. Very slowly, she raised her right arm a second time and again seemed to circle her arm—only this time her arm was lower, more at waist level. She then lowered her arm a second time, went limp, and flatlined. She died.

We all stood speechless. Then Bob looked back in our direction and said, "It was like she was hugging." I replied, "It was like two hugs." Immediately, Bob said, "Rose?" I replied, "I do not know, but her arm went up twice, the second time lower than the first." "I think it was Rose and my dad," Bob said. We stood once again in silence. All three of us had red eyes at this point and the room felt holy. We all knew we had just experienced something we would never forget and would never be able to explain. Finally, Bob broke the silence and said, "Did you see she squeezed my hand?" I admitted I had not, adding I was watching her right arm, and then concluded maybe that was a gift meant only for him.

Practical Implications

Among the practical implications of living in the mystery and in openness to experiencing the divine is a recognition of the need for a more holistic understanding of patient and family care. The article titled "Near-Death Experiences and Religious Experience: An Exploration of Spirituality in Medicine" emphasizes this need when exploring end-of-life care. Kopel and Webb summarize this need and the impact of the reality and study of NDEs, writing, "In general, viewing NDEs from a point of view informed by both science and religion may constitute a paradigm change in medical treatment, combining scientific research and belief with patient disease experiences with a new understanding of spiritual and medical relationships."[17]

The professional chaplain is an integral part of the team of caregivers in a holistic approach to care for patients, families, and loved ones. Further, one of the stated functions of the professional chaplain according to BCCI is to provide the voice of integration and the perspective of one's own faith tradition. This function is stated in BCCI competencies,

- Section III: Professional Practice Skills Competencies
- PAS7: "Provide religious/spiritual resources appropriate to the care of patients, families and staff."
- Section IV: Professional Competencies
- PRO1: "Promote the integration of Pastoral/Spiritual Care into the life and service of the institution in which it resides."[18]

Finally, it is often the professional chaplain who is the member of the team who is physically present at the end of life with patients, families, and loved ones. It is the professional chaplain who is given the role to listen in a nonjudgmental way thus creating a safe environment for those who may have experienced an NDE. Therefore, it is the professional chaplain who can provide the space for processing, healing, and integration within the patient. It is the professional chaplain who, by taking their place within the medical care team and within the care of patients and families, assists

---

17. Kopel and Webb, "Near-Death and Religious Experience," 2.
18. "Professional Chaplain Competencies," sec. 4.

the whole to live within the mystery of life and the possibility of experiences of the divine.

Spiritual Discernment Questions

1. Have you ever experienced something that cannot be explained scientifically or medically? If so, explain.
2. How might your response influence your ministry as a professional chaplain?

Chapter 6

Trailblazers: Interviews with Professional Chaplains

WEBSTER'S DICTIONARY DEFINES THE word trailblazer as "one that blazes a trail to guide others: pathfinder."[1] This chapter includes interviews with professional chaplains who reside in various evangelical voices in the Christian family. These individuals have served God and through their ministries have paved a way for those who may follow in the ministry of professional chaplaincy.

Interview 1

First name: Lynn

Church Affiliation: Nondenominational

Primary Location: Hospital

Years of Service as a Professional Chaplain: 6

What have you found most meaningful in your ministry as a professional chaplain?

Hearing and listening to people's stories.

What have you found most challenging in your ministry as a professional chaplain?

---

1. *Webster's Dictionary*, s.v., "trailblazer," last updated Dec. 25, 2024. https://www.merriam-webster.com/dictionary/trailblazers.

Self-care, because I tend to overextend myself.

Where have you seen and experienced God during your ministry as a professional chaplain?

When I am with a person who is facing a challenge and they have been serving God long enough to trust him even during the worst moments.

Interview 2

First name: Dave

Church Affiliation: Baptist

Primary Location: Hospital

Years of Service as a Professional Chaplain: 20

What have you found most meaningful in your ministry as a professional chaplain?

Being able to live my faith before people who are going through the worst day of their life. Working with staff who need an ear to listen to help them debrief after caring for patients and families going through trauma. A caring attitude with a compassionate heart.

What have you found most challenging in your ministry as a professional chaplain?

Working with staff and patients who do not have a faith basis and do not want to mention or bring up God in any way.

Where have you seen and experienced God during your ministry as a professional chaplain?

On a Friday afternoon, I was called by the nurses' station to go to room 315 as the patient and her friends were asking for a chaplain. I was not able to get to her because of several Code Blues and traumas in the emergency department. On my way home, God impressed upon me that I should go back and visit the patient in room 315. I continued on my way saying that I would see her on Monday. I could not get peace about it, and God impressed upon me again that I needed to go back and see her. I did not make it home—I turned around and went back to the hospital. When I walked in the room, the visitors and patient were crying. The patient said, "Thank you for coming. The ladies have been telling me about Jesus, but I don't know how to accept him and they can't help me. Can you?" I shared with her how she could know Jesus as her Savior and she gladly accepted him as her Savior. The patient and her friends were overwhelmed with joy! When I went back to see the patient on Monday, the nurse told me that she had died on Friday night. God nudging me was for a specific purpose at a specific time.

Interview 3

First name: Eric

Church Affiliation: Church of God (Cleveland, Tennessee)

Years of Service as a Professional Chaplain: 16

Primary Location: Hospice/Hospital

What have you found most meaningful in your ministry as a professional chaplain?

Interactions with families, patients, and staff.

Helping families transition from abnormal hope for physical healing to acceptance that death is a reality. To be part of this journey with patients and families. Any time I am present when a person transitions from mortality to immortality.

One example comes to mind. While working as a hospice chaplain I went to visit a woman I had seen before. She was close to death. I sat next to her and found the song "When He Was on the Cross." The song was playing on my work iPad. She laid her head on my left shoulder and she died.

What have you found most challenging in your ministry as a professional chaplain?

The stranglehold of executive leadership, unrealistic expectations placed on professional chaplains, and the stress that follows. The times of devaluation of professional chaplains as a profession.

Where have you seen and experienced God during your ministry as a professional chaplain?

"The Hopping, One-Legged Man"

While working a Friday night shift at a level 1 trauma hospital the team gathered in the trauma bay for a man that was being life-flighted because he had been hit by a train.

When he arrived, he was unconscious, his left leg was almost taken off below the knee and his left arm was dangling and seemed to be held only by skin. I approached the bed and held the man's hand and prayed for the patient and the staff. It was not expected that the man would survive.

When I returned to work on Monday, I was rounding my units. While rounding I saw a man in a doorway hopping on one leg and an arm in a full-cast.

I stopped and spoke with the patient. The patient laughed and said, "I thought I recognized your voice. I couldn't see your face." He then explained that he had been "high" and was playing his guitar on the tracks. He said he was "blessed because he had been running from God for years. Mama had prayed for years to the Lord, 'Whatever it takes, God save his soul! And God hit me with a train!'" We laughed hard.

Thinking about this experience I continue to be astounded that he was able to remember hearing my voice that night in the trauma bay. Everyone assumed he was unconscious and unaware of what was going on and very likely was going to die. Meeting him a few days later, hopping on one foot, and speaking with him was God. Further, I think our talking might have validated the experience to him.

I do know he is going to be telling his story—and "testifying!"—whenever he gets the chance. I can only wonder what God might do with his testimony.

Spiritual Discernment Questions

1. Which of the stories shared in this chapter sticks with you the most? Why do you think that story sticks with you and how might this influence your ministry as a professional chaplain?

2. Self-care is mentioned as a challenge by some of the "trailblazers." It is necessary for anyone who wants longevity in professional chaplaincy. What are some of your current forms of self-care? How might these grow and evolve?

Chapter 7

The Professional Chaplain as Evangelist

"... and he sent them out to proclaim the kingdom of God and to heal"

LUKE 9:2

THE TITLE, "THE PROFESSIONAL Chaplain as Evangelist" leads us to a deeper question. Professional chaplaincy at its heart is a representative ministry; therefore the question arises, Can representative ministry act as an effective tool of evangelism? Can representative ministry evangelize a people and, in some cases, elicit societal change?

To explore these questions, I will examine three events that have all occurred within the last hundred years. The first is, the witness of the four chaplains and the sinking of the USAT Dorchester. On the morning of February 3, 1943, the USAT Dorchester was struck by a German torpedo. Serving on the boat were four chaplains: John P. Washington, a Catholic priest; Alexander D. Goode, a Jewish Rabbi; George L. Fox, a Methodist minister; and Clarke V. Poling, a minister in the Reformed Church of America. During the chaos that ensued and as the Dorchester was sinking into the freezing waters of the North Atlantic, these four chaplains assisted terrified sailors off the boat and into the water. Each of these chaplains would give up their own life jacket to save the life of another. In the end, of the 904 passengers on the USAT Dorchester, only 230 survived. The four chaplains were among those who lost their lives.[1]

In literal terms the actions of these four chaplains saved four lives. However, the self-sacrifice demonstrated in representative ministry lives on well beyond their initial sacrifice.

We have the example of Aimee Semple McPherson (1890–1944), the founder of the International Church of the Foursquare Gospel. As a young woman, McPherson served as a missionary to China. Led by the Holy Spirit she began serving the needs within her own community in Los Angeles, eventually establishing the Foursquare Church, Angelus Temple, in 1923. The movement has held it a priority to go on mission, sending out missionaries to the poor. McPherson modeled the need for both evangelism as proclamation and representative ministry.[2]

On October 7, 1950, Mother Teresa received permission from the Holy See to start her own order, The Missionaries of Charity, whose primary task was to love and care for those persons nobody was prepared to look after. In the book by Mother Teresa titled *In the Heart of the World: Thoughts, Stories, and Prayers* is a writing that to me summarizes representative ministry. Mother Teresa writes,

> There is much suffering in the world—very much. Material suffering from hunger, suffering from homelessness, from all kinds of disease, but I still think that the greatest suffering is being lonely, feeling unloved, just having no one. I have come more and more to realize that it is being unwanted that is the worst disease that any human being can ever experience. In these times of development, the whole world runs and is hurried. But there are some who fall down on the way and have no strength to go ahead. These are the ones we must care about. Let us be

1. Clifford, "No Greater Glory."
2. Britannica, "Aimee Semple McPherson."

very sincere in our dealings with each other and have the courage to accept each other as we are. Do not be surprised at or become preoccupied with each other's failure; rather see and find the good in each other, for each one of us is created in the image of God. Jesus has said it beautifully: "I am the vine; you are the branches." The life-giving sap that flows from the vine through each of the branches is the same.[3]

According to the Pew Research Center, in an article written by Stephanie Kramer titled "Key findings of the religious composition in India," there were eight million Christians or 2.3 percent of the population in 1951.[4] If 2.3 percent of the current Indian population were Christian it would mean between twenty-eight million and thirty-one million Christians are living in India. However, the actual number of Christians in India may be much higher.

Philip Jenkins in his book *The Next Christendom: The Coming of Global Christianity* examines the growth of Christianity in various locations throughout the world. He writes that modest estimates say that today 6 percent of the Indian population is Christian and that its growth is occurring throughout economic, regional, and cultural backgrounds. He cites the 2000 *World Christian Encyclopedia* for this information. In the year 2000 this would have meant sixty-two million Christians in India.[5] If this 6 percent is used in the year 2022 it would mean nearly eighty-three million Christians today in India.

Whether the figure is twenty-eight million or nearly eighty-three million the growth of Christianity since 1951 has been staggering. One can only imagine the representative ministry begun by Mother Teresa in 1950 might have had on this growth in Christianity in India.

---

3. Teresa, *Heart of the World*, 14–15.
4. Kramer, "Religious Composition in India," para. 3.
5. Jenkins, *Next Christendom*, 83–84.

What is a Wildflower?

Professional chaplains serve in many different settings and in many capacities. These different settings are growing in our day. In this way, professional chaplaincy as an evangelist can be seen in Jesus' parable of a farmer who went out to sow seeds (Matt 13:3-9). These seeds landed in a variety of places and some of the seeds *fell on good soil, where it produced a crop- a hundred, sixty or thirty times what was sown. He who has ears, let them hear* (Matt 13:8-9).

A wildflower, like a professional chaplain, often goes where the wind or *spirit* leads. An example would be a hospital chaplain, where in many situations, it is impossible to see every patient and the professional chaplain asks for the *spirit* to lead them to where they need to be on a given day. In a similar way to the wildflower, the professional chaplain then seeks to bloom, add peace, and reflect God's presence wherever they are planted.

Further, like a wildflower, the professional chaplain needs to be resilient, clinging to the soil (clinging to God) for continued nourishment to weather, survive, and thrive. Any professional chaplain quickly learns the need to repeatedly return to the source of one's call to then have the ability and the physical, emotional, and spiritual energy to meet the representative ministry demands of the job.

Conclusion

This book has sought to describe the validity of the role of the evangelical in professional chaplaincy by focusing on three issues that arise as blessings of current debates within the church universal and requirements within the world of professional chaplaincy. First, requirements in the world of professional chaplaincy remind us that the world, not an individual church or denomination or even Christian believers, is our parish. The world is our parish. Second, a recommitment to serious thought and implications to the Holy Trinity reminds us that God is beyond any human thought or theology. This allows God to be God and humans to be free to be authentically human. Third, recent church debates and professional chaplaincy requirements move us to the gift of authenticity. Authenticity moves us to being defined not by what we are not but who and what we are.

This role of the evangelical chaplain in professional chaplaincy is challenging and demanding; however, working in God's vineyard (Matt 20:1–16) is always challenging and demanding. In this way, it is critical that the evangelical chaplain not concede the ministry of professional chaplaincy due to challenges that may be experienced. It is not legal to exclude the evangelical chaplain from ministry as a professional chaplain. Further, God is creating pathways to reach the unchurched in a multi-cultural society and throughout this book I have made the argument that professional chaplaincy is one of those pathways. God will bless the work of the evangelical chaplain whose ministry resides in professional chaplaincy. Therefore, it is imperative that evangelicals show up and do our part in God's vineyard.

Spiritual Discernment Questions

1. What are three blessings of current debates within the church universal and requirements within the world of professional chaplaincy?

2. After reading the handbook are there any new biblical passages or images that come to mind when considering ministry in the local church? Are there any new biblical passages or images that come to mind when considering professional chaplaincy? How might these new biblical passages and images impact your ministry moving forward?

3. Are you considering ministry as a professional chaplain rooted in representative ministry or do you feel more drawn to local church ministry rooted in proclamation ministry? Explain

Bibliography

Albom, Mitch. *Tuesdays with Morrie: An Old Man, A Young Man, and Life's Greatest Lessons.* New York: Doubleday, 1997.

Alexander, Eben. *Proof of Heaven: A Neurosurgeon's Journey into the Afterlife.* New York: Simon & Schuster, 2012.

Alexander, Neil. *The Epistles of John.* Torch Bible Commentaries. New York: MacMillan, 1962.

Allman, James E. "First John 1:9: Confession as a Test, but of What?" *Bibliotheca Sacra* 172 (Apr. 2015) 203–221.

Andrews, Mary Raymond Shipman. "The Soldiers' Angel." In *Great Lives, Great Deeds.* Pleasantville, NY: Reader's Digest Association, 1964.

Atkin, Robert K. "Critical Review, Response and Application of Reading Based on Fowler's Theory of Stages of Faith." *Robert K. Atkin* (blog), June 27, 2024. https://robertatkin.net/essays/critical-review-response-application-reading-based-fowlers-theory-stages-faith/.

Balboni, Tracy A., and J. R. Peteet. *Spirituality and Religion Within the Culture of Medicine: From Evidence to Practice.* New York: Oxford University Press, 2017.

Balboni, Tracy A., et al. "Religiousness and Spiritual Support Among Advanced Cancer Patients and Associations with End-of-Life Treatment Preferences and Quality of Life." *Journal of Clinical Oncology* 25.5 (2007) 555–60. https://doi.org/10.1200/JCO.2006.07.9046.

Bassett, Lynn. "Space, Time and Shared Humanity: A Case Study Demonstrating a Chaplain's Role in End-of-Life Care." *Health and Social Care Chaplaincy* 5.2 (2018) 194–208. https://doi.org/10.1558/hscc.34298.

Bauckham, Richard. *Bible and Mission: Christian Witness in a Postmodern World.* Grand Rapids: Baker Academic, 2003.

Beam, Christy Wilson. *Miracles from Heaven: A Little Girl and Her Amazing Story of Healing.* New York: Hachette, 2016.

Benedetti, Fabrizio. "Placebo and the New Physiology of the Doctor-Patient Relationship." *Physiological Review* 93 (2013) 1207–46. https://doi.org/10.1152/physrev.00043.2012.

Black, Clifton C., ed. *Hebrews, James, 1 & 2 Peter, 1, 2 & 3 John, Jude, Revelation.* Vol. 12 of *The New Interpreter's Bible: A Commentary in Twelve Volumes.* Nashville: Abingdon, 1998.

Blackmore, Susan. *Consciousness: An Introduction.* Oxford: Routledge, 2004.

Board of Chaplaincy Certification, Inc. (BCCI). "BCCI Competency Essay Writing Guide." May 2020. https://www.apchaplains.org/bcci-site/becoming-certified/applications-and-forms/bcci-competency-essay-writing-guide/.

———. *BCCI Competencies Rubric 2024.* Last updated Nov. 2024. https://www.apchaplains.org/bcci-site/wp-content/uploads/sites/2/2024/11/Rubric-Competencies-11-2024.pdf.

Bonanno, G. A. "Loss, Trauma, and Human Resilience: Have We Understood the Human Capacity to Thrive after Extremely Aversive Events?" *American Psychologist* 59.1 (2004) 20–28.

———. "Uses and Abuses of the Resilience Construct: Loss, Trauma, and Health-Related Adversities." *Social Science and Medicine* 74 (2012) 753–56.

Bonhoeffer, Dietrich. *Spiritual Care.* Translated by Jay C. Rochelle. Minneapolis: Fortress, 1985.

Britannica. "Aimee Semple McPherson." Last updated Nov. 25, 2024. https://www.britannica.com/biography/Aimee-Semple-McPherson.

Brown, Raymond. *The Epistles of John.* Anchor Bible 30. New York: Doubleday, 1982.

———. *The Gospel and Epistles of John: A Concise Commentary.* Collegeville, MN: Liturgical, 1988.

Brueggemann, Walter, ed. *Hope for the World: Mission in a Global Context.* Louisville: Westminster John Knox, 2001.

Cadge, Wendy, and Emily Sigalow. "Negotiating Religious Differences: The Strategies of Interfaith Chaplains in Healthcare." *Journal for the Scientific Study of Religion* 52 (2013) 146–58.

Cadge, Wendy, et al. "Training Chaplains and Spiritual Caregivers: The Emergence and Growth of Chaplaincy Programs in Theological Education." *Pastoral Psychology* 69 (June 2020) 187–208.

Callanan, Maggie, and Patricia Kelley. *Final Gifts: Understanding the Special Awareness, Needs and Communications of the Dying.* New York: Bantam, 1992.

Cant, Robyn, et al. "The Divided Self: Near Death Experiences of Resuscitated Patients—A Review of Literature." *International Emergency Nursing* 20.2 (2012) 88–93. https://doi.org/10.1016/j.ienj.2011.05.005.

Cleveland Clinic. "What Happens in Your Body When You're Lonely?" Feb. 23, 2018. https://health.clevelandclinic.org/what-happens-in-your-body-when-you-are-lonely/.

Clifford, James H. "No Greater Glory: The Four Chaplains and the Sinking of the USTA Dorchester." Army Historical Foundation. https://armyhistory.

org/no-greater-glory-the-four-chaplains-and-the-sinking-of-the-usat-dorchester/.

Collins, Adela Yardro. *Crisis and Catharsis: The Power of the Apocalypse.* Philadelphia: Westminster, 1984.

Corbitt, Otis. *An Introduction to Chaplaincy Ministry: An Evangelical Christian Perspective.* Self-published, 2020.

Crick, Robert. *Journeying with Jeanette: A Love Story into the Land and Language of Alzheimer's.* Oviedo, FL: Higher Life, 2016.

Davis, Ellen. *Wondrous Depth.* Louisville: Westminster John Knox, 2005.

Denworth, Lydia. "The Power of Purpose and Meaning in Life: A New Study Reveals the Pervasive Effects of Feeling That Life Is Worthwhile." *Psychology Today*, Jan. 12, 2019. https://www.psychologytoday.com/ie/blog/brain-waves/201901/the-power-purpose-and-meaning-in-life.

Elmore, Michael William. "Discovering an Evangelical Theology of Chaplaincy." PhD diss., Ashland Theological Seminary, 2018. https://rim.ir.atla.com/concern/etds/af8663d8-a3f2-4779-9509-a2362aeb7963.

Erzen, Tanya. *God in Captivity: The Rise of Faith-Based Prison Ministries in the Age of Mass Incarceration.* Boston: Beacon, 2017.

Flannelly, Kevin J., et al. "A National Study of Chaplaincy Services and End-of-Life Outcomes." *BMC Palliative Care* 11.10 (2012) 1–6. https://doi.org/10.1186/1472-684X-11-10.

Fowler, James W. *Becoming Adult, Becoming Christian: Adult Development and Christian Faith.* San Francisco: Jossey-Bass, 2000.

———. *Faith Development and Pastoral Care: Theology and Pastoral Care.* Minneapolis: Fortress, 1987.

Frame, Selby. "Julianne Holt-Lunstad Probes Loneliness, Social Connections." American Psychological Association. Oct. 18, 2017. https://www.apa.org/members/content/holt-lunstad-loneliness-social-connections.

Fukuyama, Mary A., and Todd Servig. "Cultural Diversity in Pastoral Care." *Journal of Health Care Chaplaincy* 1 (2008) 25–42. https://pubmed.ncbi.nlm.nih.gov/15478983/.

Fuller, Michael. "Did St. Jerome Have a Near-Death Experience?" *Expository Times.* 120.11 (2009) 530–33. https://doi.org/10.1177/0014524609106839.

Giles, Kevin. *What on Earth Is the Church? An Exploration in New Testament Theology.* Eugene, OR: Wipf & Stock, 1995.

Gomi, Sachiko, et al. "Spiritual Assessment in Mental Health Recovery." *Community Mental Health Journal* 50 (2014) 447–53.

Grant, George, et al. "Chaplains' Role in End-of-Life Decision Making: Perspectives of African American Patients and Their Family Members." *Journal of Pain and Symptom Management.* 49.2 (2015) 412–13. https://www.jpsmjournal.com/article/S0885-3924(14)00776-3/fulltext.

Grayston, Kenneth. *The New Testament: Which Way In?* London: Darton, Longman & Todd, 2000.

Bibliography

Greyson, Bruce. "Incidence of Near-Death Experiences." *Medicine & Psychiatry* 1 (Dec. 1998) 92–99. https://med.virginia.edu/perceptual-studies/wp-content/uploads/sites/360/2017/01/NDE33_incidence-MP.pdf.

Gupta, Sanjay. "Why You Should Treat Loneliness as a Chronic Illness." *Everyday Health*, Aug. 4, 2015.

Harper, Steve. *The Way to Heaven: The Gospel According to John Wesley*. Grand Rapids: Zondervan, 2003.

Harris, Elise. "African Bishops Throw Swift Punch at 'Ideological Colonization.'" *Catholic News Agency*, Oct. 8, 2015. https://www.catholicnewsagency.com/news/32785/african-bishops-throw-swift-punch-at-ideological-colonization.

Harris, Trudy. *Glimpses of Heaven: True Stories of Hope and Peace at the End of Life's Journey*. Grand Rapids: Revell, 2008.

Harvard Health Publishing. "Loneliness Has Same Risk as Smoking for Heart Disease." June 16, 2016. https://www.health.harvard.edu/staying-healthy/loneliness-has-same-risk-as-smoking-for-heart-disease#:~:text=The%20data%20showed%20that%20loneliness,obesity%2C%20according%20to%20the%20researchers.

Healthy Brains. "Loneliness and Alzheimer's—What You Should Know." Cleveland Clinic. Feb. 10, 2017. https://healthybrains.org/loneliness-alzheimers-know/.

Heinke, Gary D., et al. "Quality of Spiritual Care at the End of Life: What the Family Expects for Their Loved One." *Journal of Health Care Chaplaincy* 26.4 (2019) 159–74. https://doi.org/10.1080/08854726.2019.1644816.

Holt-Lunstad, Julianne, et al. "Social Relationships and Mortality Risk: A Meta-Analytic Review." *PLOS Medicine* 7.7 (2010) 1–20. https://doi.org/10.1371/journal.pmed.1000316.

Ince, Irwin L., Jr. *The Beautiful Community: Unity, Diversity, and the Church at Its Best*. Downers Grove, IL: InterVarsity, 2020.

Jenkins, Philip. *The Next Christendom: The Coming of Global Christianity*. Oxford: Oxford University Press, 2007.

Kärkkäinen, Veli-Matti. "Ecclesiology and the Church in Christian Tradition and Western Theology." In *The Church from Every Tribe and Tongue: Ecclesiology in the Majority World*, edited by Green et al., 15–34. Cumbria, UK: Langham Global Library, 2018.

King, Martin Luther, Jr. *Strength to Love*. New York: Pocket, 1963.

Kopel, Jonathan, and Mark Webb. "Near-Death Experiences and Religious Experience: An Exploration of Spirituality in Medicine." *Religions* 13.2 (Feb. 2022) 1–12.

Kramer, Stephanie. "Key Findings About the Religious Composition in India." Pew Research Center. Sept. 21, 2021. https://www.pewresearch.org/short-reads/2021/09/21/key-findings-about-the-religious-composition-of-india/.

Bibliography

Kress, Robert. "Unity in Diversity and Diversity in Unity: Toward an Ecumenical Perichoresic Kenotic Trinitarian Ontology." *Dialogue & Alliance* 4.3 (1990) 66–70.

Kübler-Ross, Elisabeth. *On Death and Dying: What the Dying Have to Teach Doctors, Nurses, Clergy, and Their Own Families*. London: Routledge, 1969.

Kulah, Arthur F. "The Authority of the Church." *Good News: A Magazine for United Methodist Renewal*, July/Aug. 2000, 8–12.

Kysar, Robert. *John: The Maverick Gospel*. Rev. ed. Louisville: Westminster John Knox, 1976.

Lambrecht, Thomas. "Violations in Central Congo." *Good News Magazine*, July 17, 2020. https://goodnewsmag.org/?s=Violations+in+Central+Congo.

———. "East Angola Controversy." *Good News Magazine*, Apr. 8, 2022. https://goodnewsmag.org/?s=East+Angola+Controversy.

Lang, John D. *In Jesus' Name: Evangelicals and Military Chaplaincy*. Eugene, OR: Resource, 2010.

Langness, David. "Plato, Socrates and Hieronymus Bosch on Near-Death Experiences." BahaiTeachings.org. Nov. 24, 2014. https://bahaiteachings.org/plato-socrates-and-hieronymus-bosch-on-near-death-experiences/.

Li, Shanshan, et al. "Association of Religious Service Attendance and Mortality Among Women." *JAMA Internal Medicine* 176.6 (2016) 777–85.

Lindberg, Christine A. and Benjamin G. Zimmer, eds. *Oxford American Dictionary*. 2nd ed. Oxford: Oxford University Press, 2008.

Loader, William. *The Johannine Epistles*. Epworth Commentaries. London: Epworth, 1992.

Macdonald, Gordon. "The Efficacy of Primary Care Chaplaincy Compared with Antidepressants: A Retrospective Study Comparing Chaplaincy and Antidepressants." *Primary Health Care Research & Development* 18 (2017) 354–65. https://doi.org/10.1017/S1463423617000159.

Marty, Paige K., et al. "Loneliness and ED Visits in Chronic Obstructive Pulmonary Disease." *Mayo Clinic Proceedings* 3.3 (2019) 350–57. https://doi.org/10.1016/j.mayocpiqo.2019.05.002.

Matthews-King, Alex. "Religious People Live Four Years Longer Than Atheists, Study Finds." *Independent*, June 13, 2018. https://www.independent.co.uk/news/health/religion-live-longer-muslim-jewish-christian-hindu-buddhist-life-expectancy-age-a8396866.html

McCaulley, Esau. *Reading While Black: African American Biblical Interpretation as an Exercise in Hope*. Downers Grove, IL: InterVarsity, 2000.

McDermond, J. E. *1, 2, 3 John*. Believers Church Bible Commentary. Harrisonburg, VA: Herald, 2011.

McPolin, James. *John*. New Testament Message 6. Wilmington, DE: Michael Glazier, 1979.

Miller, Lisa. "This Ivy League Researcher Says Spirituality Is Good for Our Mental Health." Interview by Rachel Martin. *All Things Considered*, NPR, July 30, 2023. https://www.npr.org/2023/07/30/1190748216/religion-spirituality-science-mental-health.

Bibliography

Moody, Raymond, Jr. *Life After Life*. Covington, GA: Mockingbird, 1976.

National Cancer Institute. "Spirituality in Cancer Care (PDQ)–Health Professional Version" Last updated Dec. 12, 2023. https://www.cancer.gov/about-cancer/coping/day-to-day/faith-and-spirituality/spirituality-hp-pdq.

Neal, Mary C. *To Heaven and Back: A Doctor's Extraordinary Account of Her Death, Heaven, Angels, and Life Again; A True Story*. Colorado Springs: WaterBook, 2011.

Nouwen, Henri. *The Wounded Healer*. New York: Doubleday, 1972.

Orlando, Alex. "Can Science Explain Near Death Experiences?" *Discover Magazine*, Aug. 23, 2021. https://www.discovermagazine.com/mind/can-science-explain-near-death-experiences.

Oyez. "Burwell v. Hobby Lobby Stores." Last updated Jan. 8, 2024. https://www.oyez.org/cases/2013/13-354.

———. "Fulton v. City of Philadelphia." Last updated Jan. 8, 2024. https://www.oyez.org/cases/2020/19-123.

———. "Kennedy v. Bremerton School District." Last updated Jan. 8, 2024. https://www.oyez.org/cases/2021/21-418.

———. "Little Sisters of the Poor Saints Peter and Paul Home v. Philadelphia." Last updated Jan. 8, 2024. https://www.oyez.org/cases/2019/19-431.

———. "Masterpiece Cakeshop, Ltd. v. Colorado Civil Rights Commision." Last updated Jan. 8, 2024. https://www.oyez.org/cases/2017/16-111.

Pargament, Kenneth I., et al. "Religion and HIV: A Review of the Literature and Clinical Implications." *Southern Medical Journal* 97.12 (2004) 1201–9.

Parker, Clifton B. "Stanford Research: The Meaningful Life Is a Road Worth Traveling." *Stanford Report*, Jan. 1, 2014.

Peattie, Donald Culross. "Everybody's Saint." In *Great Lives, Great Deeds*. Pleasantville, NY: Reader's Digest Association, 1964.

Piderman, K. M., et al. "Patient's Expectations of Hospital Chaplains." *Mayo Clinic Proceedings* 83.1 (2008) 58–65. https://doi.org/10.4065/83.1.58.

Piper, Don. *90 Minutes in Heaven: A True Story of Death and Life*. Grand Rapids: Revell, 2004.

Rensberger, David. *1, 2, and 3 John*. Abingdon New Testament Commentaries. Nashville: Abingdon, 1997.

Rey, Ariel R. "Report: Christians Live Healthier, Longer." *The Christian Post*, Apr. 25, 2011. https://www.christianpost.com/news/report-christians-live-healthier-longer.html.

Ruiz, John. *A Chaplain's Perspective on the 2020–2021 Pandemic: Tragedy, Resilience, Hope*. Seattle: BluePrint, 2021.

Ruth, Elizabeth. *Daily Readings with St John of the Cross*. Springfield, IL: Templegate, 1986.

Saad, Lydia. "One in Four Americans Have Been Served by Chaplains." Gallup. Dec. 14, 2022. https://news.gallup.com/opinion/gallup/406838/one-four-americans-served-chaplains.aspx.

Senior, Donald. *The Passion of Jesus in the Gospel of John.* Collegeville, MN: Liturgical, 1991.
Sherman, Franklin. "Dietrich Bonhoeffer." *Britannica,* last updated Jan. 7, 2025. https://www.britannica.com/biography/Dietrich-Bonhoeffer.
Sloyan, Gerald S. *John.* Interpretation. Atlanta: John Knox, 1988.
———. *Walking in the Truth: Preservers and Deserters: The First, Second, and Third Letters of John.* Valley Forge, PA: Trinity, 1995.
Spidell, Steven. "Resilience and Professional Chaplaincy: A Paradigm Shift in Focus." *Journal of Health Care Chaplaincy* 20.1 (2014) 16–24.
Spiritual Care Association. "Code of Ethics." https://www.spiritualcareassociation.org/code-of-ethics/.
Stanton, Glen T. *The Myth of the Dying Church: How Christianity Is Actually Thriving in America and the World.* New York: Worthy, 2019.
Storm, Howard. *My Descent Into Death: A Second Chance at Life.* New York: Doubleday, 2005.
Teresa, Mother. *In the Heart of the World: Thoughts, Stories and Prayers.* Edited by Becky Benenate. Novato, CA: New World Library, 1997.
———. "Nobel Lecture." The Nobel Prize. Dec. 11, 1979. https://www.nobelprize.org/prizes/peace/1979/teresa/lecture/.
Thomas, John Christopher. *1 John, 2 John, 3 John.* Pentecostal Commentary. New York: T&T Clark, 2004.
Thompson, Marianne Meye. "The Gospel of John and Early Trinitarian Thought: The Unity of God in John, Irenaeus and Tertullian." *Journal of Early Christian History* 4.2 (2014) 154–66.
Tietz, Christiane. *Theologian of Resistance: The Life and Thought of Dietrich Bonhoeffer.* Translated by Victoria J. Barnett. Minneapolis: Fortress, 2013.
Tutu, Desmond. *God Has A Dream: A Vision of Hope for Our Time.* New York: Doubleday, 2004.
Utley, Joni L., and Amy Wachholtz. "Spirituality in HIV+ Patient Care." *Psychiatry Issue Brief* 8.3 (2011) 1–3. https://www.umassmed.edu/globalassets/center-for-mental-health-services-research/documents/products-publications/issue-briefs/wellness/spirituality-in-hiv-patient-care.pdf.
Waters, Guy. "I John 2:22—What Does the Liar Deny?" *PBJ* 8.1 (2016) 29–48.
Weissbourd, Richard, et al. "Loneliness in America: How the Pandemic Has Deepened an Epidemic of Loneliness and What We Can Do About It." Making Caring Common Project, Harvard Graduate School of Education. Feb. 2021. https://mcc.gse.harvard.edu/reports/loneliness-in-america.
Williamson, Rick. *1, 2, and 3 John: A Commentary in the Wesleyan Tradition.* New Beacon Bible Commentary. Kansas City: Beacon Hill, 2010.
Wirpsa, M. Jeanne, et al. "Interprofessional Models for Shared Decision Making: The Role of the Health Care Chaplain." *Journal of Health Care Chaplaincy* 25.1 (2019) 20–44. https://doi.org/10.1080/08854726.2018.1501131.
Yarbrough, Robert W. *1–3 John.* Baker Exegetical Commentary on the New Testament. Grand Rapids: Baker Academic, 2008.

Yeh, Charlotte S. "The Power and Prevalence of Loneliness." *Harvard Health* (blog), Jan. 13, 2017. https://www.health.harvard.edu/blog/the-power-and-prevalence-of-loneliness-2017011310977?utm_source=twitter&utm_medium=socialmedia&utm_campaign=011317&utm_content=blog.

Zucker, David J., et al. "The Chaplain as an Authentic and Ethical Presence." *Chaplaincy Today* 23.2 (2007) 15–24.

www.ingramcontent.com/pod-product-compliance
Lightning Source LLC
Chambersburg PA
CBHW060412090426
42734CB00011B/2292